Getting a Grip On The Basics For Kids

By
Beth Jones

THE BASICS WITH ꞵETH

3nd Printing

Getting A Grip On The Basics For Kids
Building A Firm Foundation For The Victorious Christian Life
ISBN 978-1-68031-461-8

Copyright 2003 Beth Ann Jones

Published By Jeff and Beth Jones Ministries
P.O. Box 745
Portage, Michigan 49024
thebasicswithbeth.com

Contents

Who's Who?

This Book Is Dedicated To

My four children - Meghan, Annie, Luke and Eric.

All the kids at Valley Family Church,
and especially every child who took our first
"Getting A Grip On The Basics For Kids" class!

I pray God blesses you in every way and that you would prosper in life,
be strong and healthy in body, and super strong spiritually!
3 John 2

May you get to know Him better!
Philippians 3:10

May God's Word dwell in you richly!
Colossians 3:16

May God's Word be planted deep in your heart!
Psalm 1

May God use you and your life to influence others for Jesus!
Mark 1:17

May He mightily use you throughout the whole earth!
Matthew 28:18-20

Special Acknowledgments

All you kids from Valley Family Church ... now that many of you are grown up, married and having kids of your own ... be sure to help your kids get a grip on the basics! :)

All those who prayed for this project ... may eternal fruit be your reward!

Every person who teaches children in church, public or private schools and in home schools... God bless you, your work is more important than ever!

A Note To Parents & Childrens Ministry Teachers

We are so excited about helping kids get a grip on the basics of God's Word! This will be the first "official" Bible Study for many children and it's our goal to help children know how much God loves them by helping them learn how to use their own Bibles, looking up their own verses and discovering the revelation truths of God's Word for themselves! I am confident that children can begin to learn the Word and come into a real relationship with God, where they taste and see that the Lord is good!

We can see from Bible history, as well as from current events, that the enemy doesn't wait until children are in college to begin to lure them into a life of ungodliness and evil. The devil is working overtime to snatch children as soon as possible and he is using every form of literature, media, entertainment and business enterprise to do it! While the world is feeding our kids Internet pornography, sensuality, occult thinking and violent video games, many of us have sat on the sidelines content to sing Father Abraham with our children. We need a more proactive approach to training our children in true Christianity. In today's culture and the things they face every day, we need to equip our kids with the Word for this generation. That's one of the reasons we have written this book -- we want to arm parents, church leaders and children's workers with a tool they can use to truly help kids get a grip on the basics of God's Word. We want to help Christian kids become so comfortable in their knowledge of God that they can be bold and strong when faced with peer pressures and temptations. Why not give our kids the God advantage at an early age? That's our goal in this workbook! We want to plant the seeds of God's Word into the hearts of children so they develop strong roots and grow up to be strong, successful and prosperous in all they do!

Children will study the workbook at varying levels of understanding, so please help your child follow a comfortable pace they can enjoy. How can you help kids get the most out of "Getting A Grip On The Basics For Kids"?

Here Are Some Ideas For Parents And Children's Ministry Teachers

1. *Study with them! Make it a team event! Teach a "Get A Grip" class! We've given lots of "surplus" information in this book, so feel free to help your child keep the pace that is best for him or her.*

2. *Pray for your child. I highly encourage you to pray the prayers found in Ephesians 1:14-20 and Colossians 1:9-12 for your child each day!*

3. *I encourage you to allow your child to use the New Living Translation of the Bible for this workbook, so that they can understand the Scriptures in a language at their level.*

4. *Ask your child what they are learning and how God is speaking to their hearts as they study His Word, and help them to "do the Word" each week.*

A Note To Kids

You are about to begin a fun journey in God's Word. Did you know that Jesus loves children? The Bible is full of stories of God's love for children! Did you know God is looking for Christian kids who will stand up and be counted? God is looking for kids like you, who are so comfortable in their knowledge of God that they can be bold and strong when faced with peer pressures and temptations. God wants a close relationship with you -- He wants to help you know who you are in Christ, know how to pray, know the Word and know how to live by faith. God is looking for you! God has always looked for children He could use and there are many kids in the Bible that did mighty things for God!

Here Are Some Guidelines For You As You Study "Getting A Grip On The Basics For Kids"

First, I want you to know that you can be an on-fire, cool, smart, kind and popular kid who loves God with all your heart! You can be an example of what it's like to be a real Christian to your friends!

If you have never studied the Bible before, let me give you a quick overview:

-There are two major parts to the Bible - The Old Testament and the New Testament.

-There are 66 Books in the Bible.

-We will look up "references" in the Bible, which means we will look up the Book Name, the Chapter Number and the Verse Number. For example: Genesis 1:1 or Matthew 28:19. These are Bible references.

Pray and ask God to help you understand His Word and get to know Him better.

Set aside some time each week to do your lesson. Maybe you could use part of your Sunday afternoon to spend time with God in your Bible. Take your time to study each chapter in the workbook ... this isn't a race! Look up each verse in your own Bible and read the verses thoroughly. You might even want to underline the verse in your Bible.

Be sure to double-check your Bible references. For example, notice that there is a difference between "John" and "1 John".

Once you have looked up the verse, fill in the blanks in your workbook.

Expect God to teach you more about Himself and how much He loves you!

Here's What Kids Are Saying About Getting A Grip On The Basics For Kids!

I had a great time teaching this book to the 3rd-5th graders at Valley Family Church. We thought you'd like to hear their comments about their experience taking the "Get A Grip" class using the "Getting A Grip On The Basics For Kids" book.

Here's What Our 3rd-5th Graders Learned In "Getting A Grip On The Basics For Kids"

I learned...you can get to know God. Jessica

I learned...where I will go when I die and how I am filled with the Holy Spirit. Amber

I learned..God is always on our side and if you obey your parents you wll have a long blessed life. Brittney

I learned...how to be a stronger Christian and how to have better faith. Jacob

I learned...there are three kinds of death in the Bible. Melissa

I learned...about faith muscles. Megan

I learned...God is looking for true worshippers. Luke

I learned...you can't take credit for being saved. Ciara

I learned...the inner part of God's love more closely. Lindsey

I learned...how to learn about God. Xander

I learned...how Jesus took the stinger from the "bumble bee". Tori

I learned...fear operates the same way as faith and how awesome God is. Olivia

I learned...how to get a grip. Victor

Here's Why Our 3rd-5th Graders Recommend "Getting A Grip On The Basics For Kids"

It's a great class. You will get into the Lord better like I did. Hub

This is an awesome class for Christian kids to get to know Jesus better. Audrey

Fun and exciting way of getting to know the Lord better. Kelcey

You get taught a lot of useful things that will help you through your life. Ashley

This class has some really cool facts about the Bible! Breanna

I think this class was great. Aaron

Your kids will definitely love this class. Eric

You should never pass this down. Brandyn

The teacher is cool and it is fun. Taylor

(Thanks Taylor!)

CHAPTER 1
Becoming A Christian
"How To Live Forever With God"

A. THE BIG QUESTION

How do you know if you are a Christian? What must you do to be "saved" and on your way to heaven? Does going to church or being a good kid make you a Christian? Are you a Christian just because your parents are Christians? Does it really matter what you believe? Have you ever thought about where you will spend eternity? Where will you go after you die? God has told us how to know for sure where we will go after we die. He has given us the map to Him and to heaven in His book, the Bible. Let's look at it.

B. THE ROAD MAP TO GET TO HEAVEN

1.   John 3:16

What is God's heart toward the world?_____

What did He give us?_____

If we believe in Jesus, what does God give us?_____

2.   1 John 5:11-13

Who gives us eternal life?_____

Where is this life?_____

Who has eternal life?_____

Who doesn't have eternal life?_____

What do you have if you believe in Jesus and have Him as your Lord?_____

In your own words, what is eternal life?_____

C. DO YOU KNOW YOU HAVE ETERNAL LIFE?

Do you know for sure where you will go when you die?

__ Yes, I know that I have eternal life and I am going to heaven.

How do you know?_____

__ No, I am not sure if I have eternal life and I don't know if I will go to heaven.

If you are not sure you have eternal life, or if you have questions you would like answered, then our study in the Bible will help you to know for sure if you have eternal life.

 MY STORY: *I remember when I was 6 years old; I wondered where I would go when I died. My sisters and I would talk about it. I didn't know how to be sure I was going to heaven. We would try to figure out how long eternity was and we could never get to the end of forever. I didn't know where I was going to go when I died and it sometimes scared me or made me sad. Finally, when I was 19 years old, I found out that Jesus was the way to heaven. I asked Jesus to be the Lord of my life and to come into my heart to forgive my sins. He did! I knew that I was a Christian and that I would go to heaven when I died. It was a happy day for my heart!*

D. WHO IS JESUS?

Jesus is the most important person in history! He is more important than any president or king or any sports hero or movie star. Jesus is in a different league than any other religious leader in history. For example, many religious leaders, like Confucius, Buddha, Mohammed and others, have made claims to be prophets or teachers of God, but we believe according to the Bible that they were false prophets and false teachers. *(We live in a country where we allow others to have a free choice to believe whatever they want. We have freedom of religion. We are to respect the freedom of religious belief that others have, even when we disagree with them and believe they are wrong. We try to kindly share our beliefs with them and we allow them to make up their own minds.)*

Jesus is different from any other religious leader. Here's why. Jesus didn't claim to be only a prophet, or teacher – He claimed to be God! Jesus is God! Have you ever thought about that? God became a Man and walked on the planet He created!

MY STORY: *I am the oldest of four sisters. When we were little, we would talk about Jesus. One day we kept talking about how amazing it was that Jesus was God and that God came to his own planet. He walked on the planet He made. We really wanted to go to Jerusalem so we could walk on the dirt that Jesus walked on!*

1.　　Luke 1:68-70

　　　What does this verse tell us that God sent us?_____

2.　　John 4:24-26

　　　What is God looking for?_____

　　　What is Jesus called?_____

3.　　Colossians 1:15-17

　　　Who is Jesus the visible image of?_____

　　　How long has Jesus existed?_____

4.　　John 10:11

　　　What did Jesus call Himself?_____

　　　What does He do for people?_____

E.　WHY DO WE NEED JESUS?

We need Jesus because we have sinned. Jesus is the only One who can forgive us of our sins. Think of it this way.

 TAKING A TEST: Think about taking a test at school. What if your teacher told you that the only people that could pass the test were those who got 100%? Only the students who got every question correct could pass the test. If you took the test and missed one question, you would not pass. If you took the test and missed all the questions, you would not pass. How many people do you know who would flunk the test? What if this happened...what if your teacher said that if just one person in the class got 100% on the test, she would give everyone in the class 100%? That would be a pretty good deal, wouldn't it? If one student got all the answers correct, you would get an A! Guess what? That's why we need Jesus! All of us have flunked God's test. We have not been perfect. We needed someone else to get 100% on the test and then if we accept it, God will give us that perfect score by forgiving all our sins.

Do you see how exciting this is? We need Jesus, and thank God He wants to help us! Let's look at this.

1.   How Does God Define Sin?

God is primarily concerned with our hearts. What kind of things are going on in our hearts and coming out of our hearts? Our hearts are filled with all kinds of things that are not acceptable to God when we are not Christians, but when Jesus becomes the Lord of our hearts, He forgives all our sins and makes us acceptable to God.

a.   Mark 7:15-23

What did Jesus say would "defile" us, or mess us up? (verse 15)_____

Jesus was describing our "thought life" in verse 20 – what things make us unacceptable to God?

b.   James 4:17

When your heart or conscience tells you to do the right thing and you disobey your heart or conscience, what does God call this?_____

Think about a time you were tempted to do something that you knew was wrong, how did you handle it? How did your heart feel when you were tempted to say bad words, be mean to others, or to do something that you knew was wrong and you did it? Did you feel something "scratchy" on the inside? That was your heart or conscience trying to tell you to do the right thing. It is always a good idea to obey and follow your conscience.

LYING: Think about a time you were tempted to lie. Let's say your parents asked you a question. You knew that if you told the truth you would get in trouble, so you were being tempted to tell a lie, so that you wouldn't get in trouble. Has that ever happened to you? What was going on inside your heart? What was going on inside your mind? You were the only one who knew the truth and your conscience was trying to tell you to be honest. Here's a piece of advice: it's always better to tell the truth and follow honesty! Your heart will feel right, even if you get in trouble!

 MY STORY: *When I was growing up, my mom always said, "Honesty is the best policy." She hated lying! I knew that I would get in more trouble for lying than I would for being in trouble, so I remember at times I told the truth even when I knew it meant that I would get in trouble. I wanted my heart to be clear and not feel guilty. Anytime I told a lie, my heart felt so guilty that I would usually have to confess to my parents the truth so that my heart could feel clean again. Has that ever happened to you?*

2. What Happened When We Sinned?

    a. Isaiah 59:2

        What is the result of sin?_____

 SIN: To sin means, "to miss the mark". Have you ever shot a bow and arrow? To sin means to miss the "bull's eye" of God's perfect target. When an arrow hits any of the rings outside the bull's eye, it has missed the mark. In the same way, our sin has caused us to miss the mark of God's perfection. Did you know there is a difference between our "sin nature" and our "sinful acts"? Sinful acts are the result of our sin nature. For example, have you ever seen dandelions growing in your yard? Those pretty yellow flowers are nothing more than weeds! If you wanted to get rid of the dandelions, what would you have to do? What if you mowed the lawn, would that get rid of the dandelions? Not really. They would only be gone for a day because the dandelion root is still in the ground: dandelions will be springing up all over the yard once again! The only way to totally get rid of the dandelions is to remove them from their very roots. Think of the dandelions as our "sins" and think of their roots as the "sin nature". God's biggest concern is with our sin nature. God knows that when he changes the root, our "sin nature", that our "sins" will also change.

b.   Romans 6:23

What is the "paycheck" we get for our sins?_____

What free gift does God give us when we believe in Jesus?_____

 DEATH: Death is not a pleasant topic to discuss. For many people, talking about death is a sad and scary subject. The good thing is that Jesus came to take away the sadness and scariness of death. The Bible describes three types of death: spiritual death, physical death and eternal death. These are big topics, so we will just introduce them to you now. Physical death is what happens when a person stops breathing and their heart or brain stops functioning. Physical death is when a person's body dies. Spiritual death is when a person is separated from God. If a person is not born again and doesn't know Jesus as his/her personal Lord, then that person is spiritually dead. To be spiritually dead means that a person is separated from God. Eternal death is the final condition of all those who don't know Jesus as their Lord. They will be separated from God for eternity.

3.   How Many People Sin?

Romans 3:22-26

We are made right in God's sight when we do what?_____

How many of us have sinned? (verse 23) _____

God declared that we are not guilty because Jesus did what for us?_____

F.   JESUS HAD TO DIE FOR PEOPLE LIKE US

Jesus died for people just like you and me. We might look like nice kids, and we may even go to church, but apart from Jesus we really are empty and sinful. Jesus came to solve the sin problem once and for all in order to give us a new forgiven heart; but He had to give His life in order to do that. Jesus died upon a cross and gave His life so that we could have eternal life.

Romans 5:6-11

How did God show us His great love?_____

Since we have been made right in God's sight, what are we saved from?_____

How does this make you feel in your heart?_____

BUMBLE BEES: Have you ever been stung by a bee? It hurts, doesn't it? Did you know that after a bumble bee stings you, it dies? Did you know that some people are allergic to bee stings? If they get stung, it can kill them. Imagine you were allergic to bumble bee stings and one day you and your dad are driving in your car when suddenly a bumble bee flew in the car! How would you feel? What if your dad saw the bumble bee and he put his arm out so that the bumble bee would land on him and sting his arm, instead of yours? That would sure be a loving dad, wouldn't it? If the bumble bee stung your dad, it would hurt him, but it would also take the stinger out of the bee and the bee would die! Then, you would be safe! Did you know that Your Heavenly Father loves you and He did just that? We were allergic to the sting of sin and it would cause us to die and be separated from our Heavenly Father. God sent Jesus to earth to take the sting of sin and death for us. When Jesus died on the cross for us, it was like He was stung by the "bee of sin" and He took all the pain for us. When He did this, He also took the "sting of death" away and now everyone who believes in and receives Jesus will never die, but they will spend eternity in Heaven with Him!

G. JESUS ROSE FROM THE DEAD

Do you know what we celebrate on Easter? Jesus Christ is Risen! He's not in the tomb. The tomb is empty because Jesus is alive!

a.   1 Corinthians 15:3-6

Jesus died for our sins and He was buried. What happened on the third day?_____

How many people saw Jesus after He was risen from the dead?_____

b.   Matthew 28:1-10

What happened after they put Jesus in the tomb?_____

8

Describe this story in your own words:_____

 MY STORY: *When I was in third grade, God filled my heart with a song about Jesus being risen from the dead. Has God ever put a song in your heart? I'll bet He has. Be sure to sing those songs to God. If you remember the words, write them down. God is blessing you with words from heaven! When I look back to third grade, when I was around 8 or 9 years old, God was filling my heart with songs from heaven. I was looking outside at the sunny, blue-sky day and I started to sing this song:*

> *The hills are sunny, the flowers are in bloom,*
> *The bees buzz around us, the birds fly by.*
> *The air is clean and the grass grows green,*
> *The children are playing in the sun.*
> *They are rejoicing for Jesus has risen,*
> *They are happy for what He did.*
> *He has picked this day to wash our sins away,*
> *Jesus Christ has risen.*

H.   JESUS IS THE ONLY WAY TO GOD

Jesus is God's only Savior. There is no one that can replace Him. He is the most important person in all of creation. Let's look at this.

1.   Matthew 7:13-14

How did Jesus describe the entrance to God's kingdom?_____

How did Jesus describe the highway to hell?_____

2.   John 14:6

Jesus said He was the_____, the _____ and the _____.

Who can go to the Heavenly Father without Jesus?_____

3.   Acts 4:12

Is there any other name, besides Jesus, that people can call on to be saved?_____

4. 1 Timothy 2:5

   How many mediators are there between God and man?_____

   Who is the Mediator?_____

5. Ephesians 2:1-10

   This passage summarizes everything we have discussed in this section and describes the reason we need Jesus.

   What was the result of our sin?_____

   What did God do for us?_____

   Can we take any credit for being saved?_____

   What does God call "salvation"?_____

   What does God call us?_____

   Can you see that God has a plan for your life now that you are a Christian?_____

I.   JESUS WILL GIVE US A NEW LIFE

1. 2 Corinthians 5:17

   When we believe in Jesus and receive Him into our lives, we become Christians.

   What happens to us when we become Christians?_____

   What type of life has begun?_____

2. John 3:1-7

   Jesus told Nicodemus that a person cannot see the kingdom of God unless he is what?

   _____

BORN AGAIN: Being born again is also called the "new birth". When you are born again, you don't go back into your mother's tummy to be born again, but your heart is born again! God gives you a brand new heart (or spirit) and now from your heart you can be friends with God. God welcomes you into a new Father/child relationship with Him. You are actually adopted into the family of God. You become a child of God and a member of His family when you accept Jesus as your Lord and are born again. Maybe you have a very loving mom and dad or step-parents and a wonderful family, and when you become a born-again Christian you'll get to be in God's family, too! Maybe you don't have a very happy family. Maybe your parents are divorced and you are being raised by a single parent in a difficult family situation. Maybe your home life makes you feel sad sometimes. Just remember when you become a born-again Christian, you become a member also of God's loving, healthy family and He really cares about you!

3.   John 1:12-13

Who gets to become a child of God?_____

J.   HOW DO I RECEIVE JESUS?

You can receive Jesus into your life by simply inviting Him to come into your heart. Have you ever heard your friends knock on the door of your house? When you heard the knock, what did you do? You opened the door and invited them inside, right? It's the same way with Jesus. He is knocking on the door of your heart and He wants you to answer His knock and invite Him into your life. When you receive Jesus as your Lord, you become a "Christian"! You are "saved."

 CHRISTIAN: This really means to be a follower of Christ. Acts 11:26 tells us about the first believers in the New Testament, who were called Christians.

 SAVED: Generally, this means to save, to keep safe and sound, to rescue from danger or destruction, to deliver or protect, heal, and preserve. When we accept Jesus as our Lord, we are saved from the penalty of our sin. We are saved from hell.

1.   Revelation 3:20

What is Jesus doing?_____

What does He want us to do?_____

If we open the door to Jesus, what will He do?_____

2.   John 3:16

Who can believe in Jesus?_____

What are the results of believing?_____

3.   Romans 10:8-10

Salvation comes from trusting whom?_____

What are you supposed to confess with your mouth?_____

What are you supposed to believe in your heart?_____

What are the results?_____

4.   Matthew 10:32,33

What does Jesus promise if you publicly acknowledge Him?_____

Did you know that God wants you to believe in Jesus from your heart, and He also wants you to say that Jesus is your Lord with your mouth?

 CONFESS: To confess means to agree with God or to say that same thing about Jesus that God says. To confess our belief in Jesus means to agree and to say that Jesus is Lord. Confessing Jesus as Lord means that you are saying He is your Lord.

K.   JUST DO IT - TAKE ACTION

Now it's time to just do it! Let's take action on what we have studied. Are you a Christian? Are you certain that if you were to die today you would spend eternity with God? Would you like to make the decision to invite Jesus to be the Lord of your life? Would you like Jesus to forgive you of all your sins and give you a brand new heart? Answer these two questions before we pray.

1.   Do you believe that Jesus is Lord? _____

2.   Do you believe that God raised Jesus from the dead?_____

If you answered "yes" to these two questions, you are ready to ask Jesus to be the Lord of your life by inviting Him into your life. When you ask Jesus into your life, you will be totally changed on the inside: in your heart. It's sort of like the caterpillar that is changed into a beautiful butterfly. God wants everyone to make this change. He wants you to become a beautiful Christian full of His life. If you have never asked Jesus into your heart before, would you like to do that now? This is the most important decision you will ever make in this life on the earth.

Asking Jesus into your heart means you can spend eternity, forever with Him now and in heaven. He wants to be your best friend and Lord, and help you with everything you do. He wants to be in the driver's seat, behind the steering wheel of your life. When you invite Him into your life, He will give you a new heart and wash away all your sins. He will become your closest friend. Are you ready to invite Jesus into your life? Let's pray this prayer together to invite Jesus to be your Lord and Savior.

"Dear God, I come to You and I know that I need You. I have sinned and I need Your forgiveness. Jesus, I believe that You died for me on the cross and I believe that God raised You from the dead. I believe that You are Lord Jesus, and I invite you into my heart to be the Lord of my life. I thank You for forgiving all my sins and giving me a brand new heart. I am now Your child. I am born again. I am saved and now I know I will spend forever in heaven with You when I die. Thank You, Heavenly Father. Thank You, Jesus. Amen."

Congratulations! This is the most important decision you have ever made! Jesus is now the Lord of your life! In the rest of this study, we will learn how to get to know Him better. If this is the first time you prayed a prayer to receive Jesus as your Lord, let's write it down!

Today, _____ (day/date), at _____(time)

I _____(name) prayed to receive Jesus as my Lord.

Signed:_____(your name)

Witness:_____(your parents/other)

MY PERSONAL WALK WITH GOD
Pages You Can Personalize!

The Two Most Important Dates In My Life:

The Day I Was Born On The Earth

My Birthday:

The Day I Was Born Again And Became A Christian

My Born-Again Birthday:

My Testimony

Before I asked Jesus to be the Lord of my life, this is what I remember thinking and feeling:

When I asked Jesus to be the Lord of my life, this is how it happened:

After I asked Jesus to be the Lord of my life, here's what happened:

When I Was A Baby

I was born on:

Time:

Where:

City/State:

I weighed in @:

I was this tall:

My first word was:

I took my first steps on:

CHAPTER 2
Being Sure You Are A Christian
"How To Know For Sure You're Going To Heaven"

Are you sure you are a Christian? Have you ever had any doubts? If you've had doubts, you are normal! One of the enemy's first tricks is to try to make you doubt that you are a Christian. He will try to plant thoughts in your mind to make you <u>think</u> or <u>feel</u> as though you are not really a sincere Christian. One day you may really *think* you are a born-again Christian and the next day you may not, so you can see that your "thinking" is not a good judge to go by. The enemy may also try to make you feel as if you are not saved. One day you may really *feel* like a Christian. You may feel really happy or maybe you cried tears as you responded to an altar call one day, but the next day you may feel as if you are not saved and not in God's presence. So, your "feelings" are not a good judge to go by either. Do you get the idea?

Have you ever had any doubts about being a Christian?_____

What did you do to combat those doubts?_____

How do you know that you are truly a born-again Christian? How do you know that you will live forever with God in heaven when you die? How do you come against the enemy when he works against your mind and feelings? The first thing you need to know is that your being a Christian or your salvation is based on the fact of what God has said in His Word, not on your brain's thoughts or emotional feelings.

You must go by the facts, not feelings or thoughts! Facts do not change. What are the facts? God's Word contains the unchanging facts. God's Word, the Bible, is the only authority for your Christian life. God knows every fact; His Word contains the facts. We do not depend upon feelings or emotions to be Christians, born again or saved; we are Christians, born again and saved by placing our trust, or our faith, in God and His Word. Let's take a "test" to remind ourselves that we are truly Christians. We are born again. We are saved.

A.   TAKE THE "I KNOW I AM A CHRISTIAN" TEST

1.   Facts

Does the Bible or Bible facts ever change?_____

2.   Feelings

Do our feelings ever change?_____

What determines how we feel?_____

3.   Faith

What happens if our faith or our trust is in our feelings?_____

What happens if our faith or trust is in the fact of God's Word?_____

MY STORY: *One of the best stories I have ever heard to describe the difference between fact, faith and feelings is about a train. Imagine three train cars…an engine we call "Fact", a caboose we call "Feelings", and a middle car we call "Faith". In order for the train to run down the track, the engine must pull it, right? Don't you think it would be impossible to pull the train by the caboose? In the same way, our Christian life is pulled down the track when we place our faith in the facts of God's Word. We don't pull our Christian life down the track by the caboose by placing our faith in our feelings. Some days our feelings will be up and some days our feelings will be down, so it is not a good idea to let the caboose of feelings direct our lives! We need to just choose to put our faith in the facts of God's Word and our lives will stay on track!*

B.   WHAT ARE THE FACTS WE BELIEVE?

1.   1 John 5:11-13

How do you know that you have eternal life?_____

2.   John 1:12

How do you know you became a child of God?_____

3.   Colossians 1:14

What do you know you have received for your sins?_____

4.   2 Corinthians 5:17

What have you become as a Christian?_____

What has happened to the old you?_____

5.   Romans 8:16

Who speaks to our hearts to tell us that we are God's children?_____

6.   Hebrews 13:5

What do you know that Jesus Christ will never do?_____

C.   JUST DO IT – TAKE ACTION

Now it's time to just do it! Let's take action on what we have studied.

Are you sure that you are a Christian?_____

How do you know you are a Christian - on what authority do you base your certainty?

_____

On the inside cover of your Bible (or somewhere you can keep a permanent record), write down the date and the time you received Jesus as your Lord. You may have to guess on the date and time if it was a long time ago. (You can ask your mom or dad if they remember the time you first invited Jesus to be your Lord.) Whenever the enemy tries to confuse you or discourage you with doubts about being a Christian, born again or saved, just tell him the date and time you invited Jesus Christ to be your Lord.

Once again, let's write down this important information! If you need a reminder, just look back at the end of Chapter 1.

The Date I Became A Christian By Asking Jesus Into My Heart:_____

The Location and Time:_____

Who Was With Me:_____

MY PERSONAL WALK WITH GOD
Pages You Can Personalize!

I Know I Am A Christian Because...

...God's Word tells me so...
Draw a picture of your Bible

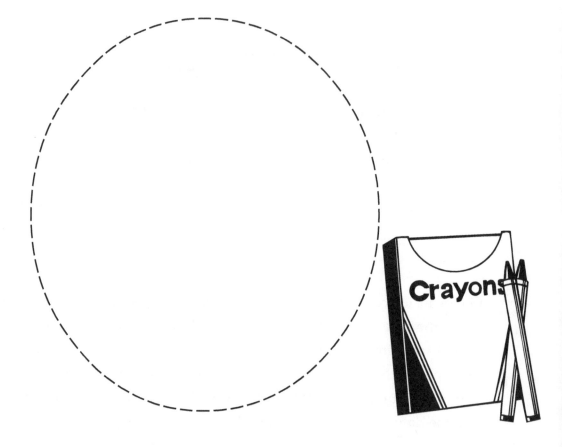

...I like to pray and talk to God...
Draw a picture of you praying

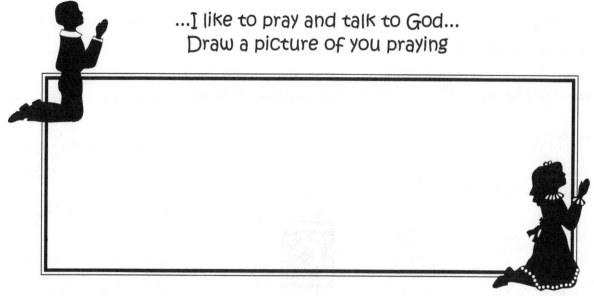

CHAPTER 3
Getting To Know God
"How To Know The Lord As Your Best Friend"

A. WHAT IS GOD LIKE?

When you become a Christian you begin a personal relationship with God. He is a Person – **not a force, or vapor, or power, or an invisible eye.** He wants to talk to you, and He wants you to talk to Him. God loves you and He wants to be your very best friend. Think about your friends. When you meet new friends, it takes many hours of talking, playing and hanging out to really get to know them, doesn't it? God has become your friend, and He is the most interesting and loving person you will ever know. Now it's going to take time, the rest of your life, to get to know and enjoy your very own personal relationship with God - Your Heavenly Father, Jesus your Lord, and the Holy Spirit your Helper.

Did you know the deep heart desire of every person is to know God? Every person has a built-in spiritual hunger that only God can satisfy. The primary ways to get to know God are spending time talking to Him in prayer (which we will look at in our next lesson), and spending time letting Him talk to you from His Word, the Bible (which we will look at in a future lesson.)

Let's take a few moments to see what your new friend is like. He has revealed Himself in the Bible. How do the following verses describe God?

1.   Who Is God?

        Matthew 28:19

        There is only one God, but He reveals Himself in three persons. That makes our brains go "tilt", doesn't it? Let's look at which three persons make up the Godhead (or Trinity).

        God the_____

        God the_____

        God the _____

2.	What do these verses tell us about God as our Father?

    a.	Matthew 7:11

        God the Father is the giver of_____

    b.	John 4:24

        God is a_____

    c.	James 1:17

        Whatever is good and perfect comes from God above.

        He never_____

3.	What do these verses tell us about Jesus our Lord?

    a.	John 8:12

        Jesus is_____

    b.	John 10:14

        Jesus is a good_____

    c.	Hebrews 13:8

        Jesus is the same_____, _____ and _____

4.	What do these verses tell us about the Holy Spirit?

    a.	1 Corinthians 3:16

        The Holy Spirit lives where?_____

b.   John 14:26

The Holy Spirit will _____ me all things

The Holy Spirit will _____ me of all things Jesus has told me

c.   John 16:13, 14

The Holy Spirit _____ me into all the truth

He _____ me things that will happen in the future

d.   Romans 8:14

The children of God are _____ by the Holy Spirit

e.   Romans 8:16

The Holy Spirit speaks to our hearts and tell us what?_____

B.   WHO ARE WE?

God made us! We were created in the image and likeness of God. God is a three-part being – Father, Son and Holy Spirit - and He has made us to be a three-part person.

1 Thessalonians 5:23

What three things, that make up the three parts of a human being, does God want to be kept blameless?

_____, _____ and _____

Our **spirit** is also called the heart, the inner man or the hidden man of the heart. Our spirit is the real, deep down inside person we are! The person who lives behind your eyes, the real you, is a spirit. **Your spirit or heart is the part of you that only you and God know!** Our spirit is the part of us that really connects with God – it's the part of us that God talks to and lives in.

Our **soul** is our personality and includes our mind, our will and our emotions. Our soul is the part of us that thinks mental thoughts and expresses our emotions of joy or tears, and our will is the part of us that makes decisions to do things or to not do things. Our soul is the part of us that learns and studies and is filled with knowledge.

Our **body** is what you look at in the mirror! It's like the "house" our spirit and soul live in. Our body is our "earth suit". Our body is the part of us that has the five physical senses of sight, hearing, taste, touch and smell that help us live in the natural world.

God wants us to be led by our spirits, but sometimes have you noticed that your soul (mind, emotions and will) and your body fight your spirit? In other words, in your heart or spirit you know the right things to do, but your mind may try to convince you to do wrong things; or your feelings may not want to do the right thing, or your body may want to pull you in another direction. You have to choose with your will to allow your spirit to win!

 APOLOGIZING: For example, have you ever been mean to someone, maybe to your brother or sister? Did your heart or spirit tell you that you should apologize to them? Did you feel like apologizing? Did you want to apologize? Now you have a choice to make. You can let your feelings dominate you, or you can let your spirit or heart dominate you. If you choose to let your spirit lead you, you will apologize and you will have peace in your heart. If you choose to let your soul or body win out, you will feel unrest in your heart, and maybe even anger. It's always best to obey and follow your heart or spirit.

It's helpful to understand that we are a three-part person, isn't it? God wants us to grow strong in our spirits by knowing Him and His Word. He wants us to fill our souls with His Word, too, so that our thoughts and emotions and will are balanced, healthy and at peace. He wants our bodies to be strong and healthy too, so that he can bless our whole life.

C. HOW DO I GET TO KNOW GOD BETTER?

1. Be Like Enoch

Did you know that Enoch was a friend of God? God liked Enoch a lot. The name Enoch means "dedicated". Enoch was dedicated to God. Let's look at his life.

a. Genesis 5:23-24

How long did Enoch live?_____

Can you imagine that?

What type of relationship did he have with God?_____

God loved Enoch so much that Enoch didn't even die! In the Old Testament, God just lifted Enoch off planet Earth and took him to heaven!

b. Hebrews 11:5

What did God think about Enoch?_____

2. Put God First In Your Life

Matthew 6:33

What does God want you to put first in your life?_____

What will God do for you, if you put Him and His kingdom first?_____

3. Love God With Your Whole Heart

Have you ever felt loved by your parents or family or friends? Did it make you feel good to know that someone loved you from their heart? Did you know that God likes it when we love Him with our whole heart? In fact, God's eyes are searching the whole earth to find people with hearts totally in love with Him. Will His eyes find you?

a. 2 Chronicles 16:9

What are God's eyes doing?_____

Who is He looking for?_____

What will He do for those who are fully committed to Him?_____

b.   Psalm 119:2

Describe the people who seek after God with their whole heart?_____

c.   Jeremiah 29:11-13

What kind of plans does He have for you?_____

If you seek God earnestly, or with your whole heart, what will you find?_____

d.   Hebrews 11:6

What does God do for those who sincerely seek Him?_____

C.   JUST DO IT – TAKE ACTION

Now it's time to just do it! Let's take action on what we have studied. Did you know that you are never too young to seek the Lord? God has a mighty plan for your life and if you will put Him first and spend time getting to know Him, you can be just like the young kids of the Bible who knew God. No matter how old you are, you can know God deeply! God will cause you to be a leader among your friends if you will put Him first. Let's look at several examples of young people that sought God!

1   Luke 2:41-52

How old was Jesus in this story?_____

What was Jesus discussing with the older religious teachers? (verse 46)_____

What do you think Jesus meant in verse 49?_____

How did Jesus respond to his parents in verse 51?_____

How did Jesus grow according to verse 52?_____

2.   Luke 1:26-38

Mary was a single, engaged young girl when God chose her to be the mother of His Son! What an honor! What if Mary had been a rebellious, backslidden teenager? Mary was an obedient, sweet-spirited young lady.

What did the angel Gabriel say to Mary in verse 28?_____

What did Mary say in verse 38?_____

3.   1 Timothy 4:12

Is this verse talking about an old person or a young person?_____

Even though you are young, God is instructing you to be an example.

In what areas are you to be an example?

_____

4.   Genesis 37:1-7

God gave a young man a dream that described God's plan for his life.

How old was Joseph when God gave him a special dream?_____

5.   2 Kings 11:21; 12:2

How old was Jehoash when he became a king?_____

What did the Lord think of Jehoash?_____

6.   2 Kings 15:1-3

How old was Azariah when he became a king?_____

What did the Lord think of Azariah?_____

7.   2 Kings 21:1-2

How old was Manasseh when he became a king?_____

What did the Lord think of Manasseh?_____

8.   2 Kings 22:1-2

How old was Josiah when he became a king?_____

What did the Lord think of Josiah?_____

9.   2 Kings 24:8-9

How old was Jehoiachin when he became a king?_____

What did the Lord think of Jehoiachin?_____

10.   2 Chronicles 26:1-5

How old was Uzziah when he became a king?_____

What did the Lord think of Uzziah?_____

As long as Uzziah sought the Lord, what did God do for him?_____

MY PERSONAL WALK WITH GOD
Pages You Can Personalize!

I Am A Spirit, I Have A Soul, I Live In A Body

My Spirit or Heart:
Draw all the things you love in your heart:

I really sense the
Lord's Presence
when...

My favorite Bible verse(s) are:

When I think about my parents,
or my family it makes me feel...

I am most at peace when...

If I had to describe how I feel in my heart about the
Lord in one sentence, here's what I'd say:

My Soul - My Mind, Emotions and Will:
Answer these questions that describe your soul...

My personality is best described as:

- ❑ a leader
- ❑ outgoing
- ❑ easy going
- ❑ creative

When I cry....

- ❑ my nose runs
- ❑ my face gets blotchy
- ❑ my body shakes
- ❑ my ears turn red

When I laugh it sounds like...
a pig snorting ❑
a bird chirping ❑
a duck quacking ❑
a cow mooing ❑

I will marry someone who...

loves the Lord ❑
is pretty or handsome ❑
likes to brush their teeth ❑
listens to Christian music ❑
all of the above ❑

My definition of a warm, fuzzy is:

I like to learn by...

doing ❑
reading ❑
listening ❑
seeing ❑
all of the above ❑

My favorite sports or activities are...circle all the ones you like:

soccer	basketball	football	baseball
ballet	skiing	computers	skateboarding
singing	dance	painting	drawing
scuba diving	swimming	acting	riding bikes
video games	surfing	checkers	snowboarding

My Body
Answer these questions that describe your body...

When I sneeze...

❑ I close my eyes
❑ I sneeze 3 times in a row
❑ I say "achoo"

I can wiggle my...

❑ ears
❑ eyebrows
❑ nose
❑ toes

This is my
self-portrait:

What color...

❑ are your eyes?_____
❑ is your hair?_____
❑ is your skin?_____

If I could change anything on
my body it would be:

I counted all my freckles
and I have this many:

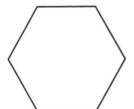

CHAPTER 4
Talking To God
"How To Pray"

Prayer is simply talking to God, from your heart. You can talk to God about anything and everything, just like you would talk to your parents or your best friend. Through praying to the Lord you will develop a really close relationship with Him.

Have you ever thought about it? When you pray, you have a meeting with the God of the Universe! You are talking to the King of kings and the Lord of lords! He is also your very own Heavenly Father. Wow! Isn't that wonderful?

The devil doesn't like prayer! He doesn't want you to get close to God. He will try to distract you from praying by keeping you too busy with other things. You need to make a decision to talk to your Heavenly Father often during the day, whether you're at home, at school or any other place. If you will do this, prayer will become as natural to you as breathing.

Let's look at how we can pray.

A.   JESUS PRAYED

1.   Mark 1:35

        When did Jesus pray?_____

        Where did He go to pray?_____

2.   Luke 6:12

        Where did Jesus go to pray?_____

        How long did He pray?_____

        Wow! That's a long time to pray isn't it? Jesus loved God so much and wanted to spend time talking to Him. He needed to get alone so He could talk to His Father.

        Do you have a special place you like to pray?_____

3.   Matthew 6:6

Where did Jesus tell us to pray?_____

You might not have a closet to pray in, but the idea is to find a quiet place that you can shut out the distractions and noise of the world around you so that you can be alone with your Heavenly Father. That might be in your bed under your covers! It could be in a special place in your home. It might be a tree fort. It could be the bathtub! Anywhere you can be alone with the Lord is a great place to pray and talk to God!

Who do we pray to?_____

What will God do in response to our prayers?_____

B.   ATTITUDES IN PRAYER

God wants you to pray from your heart; that is the most important thing. What is the main thing you learn from each of these verses?

1.   Psalm 5:1-3_____

2.   Psalm 62:8_____

Did you know that "praise and worship" is a special kind of prayer? It's the kind of prayer that God is looking for. What does this verse tell us about this kind of prayer?

3.   John 4:23-24_____

C.   GOD PROMISES TO ANSWER YOUR PRAYER

1.   Matthew 7:7-11

What does God want us to do?_____

If we ask, seek and knock, what will God do?_____

What type of gifts will our Heavenly Father give to those who ask?_____

2.   1 John 5:14

If we ask for anything in line with God's will, is He is listening?_____

If we know He is listening, what can we be sure of?_____

Did you know that God's Word tells us what God's will is? If you want to know if something is in line with God's will, look in the Bible to see what God has already told us about His will. The more you read God's Word, the more you will think like God thinks and you will know His will. While you are growing up spiritually, you should also ask your parents or pastor or more mature Christians to help you see God's will in His Word.

 MY STORY: *Let me give you an example. There are times that my children want me to buy them certain toys or games. Have you ever wanted your parents to buy you a special toy? Sometimes, even though I wanted my child to have that toy, we didn't have enough money at that moment to purchase it. I told my children that they should pray about it and ask the Lord to provide it for them. I knew this would be a good chance for them to learn how to pray faith-filled prayers and a great opportunity for them to see how good and generous God is. Here are two stories that will inspire you to seek the Lord when your parents can't afford to purchase everything your heart desires. Before, I tell you my story, let me remind you that it's important that you have a sincere and obedient heart toward God when you ask Him for things. Just like your parents, God does want to bless His children; but just like your parents, God is not interested in satisfying the desires of a whiney, spoiled, selfish child. He's listening for your childlike faith and thankfulness. Here are our stories:*

 MEGHAN AND ANNIE'S STORY: *Years ago, my daughters Meghan and Annie each wanted an American Girl doll. At the time, we couldn't afford to buy them these dolls, but we knew God had the ability to provide them with one. I knew my girls had been living obedient lives to their parents and had good hearts towards the Lord, so I prayed with them about this. We went to the Lord and we thanked Him for being a good God who gives good gifts. We asked the Lord for the American Girl dolls they wanted. We thanked the Lord by faith that He heard our prayer and since we knew He heard us, we knew we had the American Girl dolls we requested. I told my girls that from that point on, whenever they thought of the American Girl dolls they should just thank God for their dolls and in His timing, they would have them. I also challenged my girls to give something that was valuable to them as a seed sown into someone else's life. Well, can you guess what happened? In a few months, out of the blue, God opened up an opportunity for me so that I received several hundred dollars and it was just enough to purchase the two dolls, their accessories and the shipping! My girls saw first hand that their Heavenly Father is a good Father and He gives good gifts to those who ask.*

LUKE'S STORY: *A few years ago, one of our sons, Luke, wanted a Game Boy. Again, at the time we couldn't afford to buy him a Game Boy, but we knew God had the ability to provide him with one. He had been living a life pleasing to the Lord, so I prayed with him about this. We went to the Lord and we thanked Him for being a good God who gives good gifts. We asked the Lord for the Game Boy he wanted. We thanked the Lord by faith that He had heard our prayer and since we knew He heard us, we knew we had the Game Boy we requested. I told my son that from that point on, whenever he thought about the Game Boy he should just thank God for the game and in His timing, he would have the Game Boy. I also challenged my son to think about giving something valuable to others as a seed sown into others' lives. Do you want to know what happened? First, my son had been saving up "Bible Bucks" from church. This is "money" kids earn in Children's Church when they bring their Bibles to church, when they know their memory verses, etc. One day at church they received an offering for needy people and my son gave all of his Bible Bucks in that offering. Did he get the Game Boy right after giving away all his Bible Bucks? Nope! My son began to grow impatient as several months passed and no Game Boy. We just encouraged him to continue to thank God if he really believed that God had heard his original prayer, and that God was working on it. A few more months passed and no Game Boy! This was a real test of being thankful and patient! He continued to thank the Lord for his Game Boy even when he was feeling impatient! After about nine months had passed, guess what happened? One of the guest speakers we had at our church, who didn't know our son, felt "impressed by God" to give our son $100 dollars! This person didn't know what our son had prayed about! When Luke saw the $100 dollar bill, his face lit up! That week Luke took that one hundred dollars God gave him and bought the Game Boy! God knows how to answer the prayers of kids! He is a good Father!*

I hope you notice a few things from these stories. First, do you see the importance of having the right heart and attitude before God? Do you see the need to ask and have a thankful heart – even when you grow impatient? Do you see the importance of looking for ways to be a blessing and give to others when you are expecting God to bless you? Do you see the need to be patient? Can you see that every situation is unique and God knows just how to answer your request?

D.   WHEN SHOULD WE PRAY?

1.   1 Thessalonians 5:17

        When should we pray?_____

2.   Philippians 4:6-7

        Are we supposed to worry?_____

What are we supposed to do when we are tempted to worry?_____

After we tell God our need, what are we supposed to do?_____

What will God do?_____

E.   WHO SHOULD WE PRAY FOR?

1.   1 Timothy 2:1-4

Who should we pray for in this passage?_____

Who is our President?_____

Who else is an authority over you?_____

_____

2.   Ephesians 6:18

Who should we pray for?_____

3.   Matthew 9:35-38

Jesus loves everyone so much! He doesn't want anyone to be hurting or lost without Him. When He looked at the world, He saw a garden of people ripe and ready, but something was wrong.

What was wrong?_____

What did Jesus tell us to pray for?_____

4.   Luke 6:28

This is a challenge sometimes!

Who are we supposed to pray for?_____

Praying is such an honor! Just think, when you talk to your Heavenly Father and pray to Him about things and for people, He answers your prayer! Other people will be blessed because you prayed. Your own life will be blessed because you prayed. Maybe you will want to make a list of people you have on your heart to pray for. Can you think of five people in your heart you would like to pray for?

Write down their names:

_____

F.   WHAT MESSES UP OUR PRAYERS

Sometimes we need to make an adjustment in our hearts for our prayers to work the way God wants. Let's look at a few things the Lord tells us.

1.   Psalm 66:18

        What makes God not listen to our prayers?_____

        If we want to keep on sinning, God will not be able to answer our prayers.

2.   Mark 11:25

        When we are praying, what are we supposed to do if we have a grudge or unforgiveness towards someone?

        _____

Did you know that you will feel "icky" inside your heart if you have been disobedient to your parents, fought with your friends, brothers or sisters, have been mouthy to others, had a moody, bad attitude, or held a grudge against someone? If you were honest, you would notice that there is a scratchy feeling in your conscience. What do you need to do when things like this happen? First, talk to the Lord and apologize to Him. Second, apologize to anyone you have been mean or disobedient toward. Then third, forgive anyone who has been mean to you. Once you apologize and forgive, your heart will feel so much better and God will be able to answer your prayers.

G. JUST DO IT - TAKE ACTION

You might want to start keeping a Prayer Diary or a Prayer Journal where you can write letters of prayer to the Lord. Have you ever written a letter to the Lord? All you need is a pencil or pen and a notebook and you can begin!

 MY STORY: *I kept a journal when I was first a Christian. Each day I would write a short letter to the Lord to praise and thank Him for blessing my life, to ask Him for help in specific areas of my life, and to pray for the people He had put on my heart. When I was 19 years old and a student in college, I started writing letters to the Lord in my journal. Here is one of the first letters I wrote to the Lord when I was just a baby Christian.*

> *Winter 1978*
>
> *Dear God,*
>
> *Hi, this sure feels funny writing to You. Ok, first I want to clear up some things. I'm really deeply sorry for my sins and You know what they are. Even my thoughts sometimes I'm sorry for. I want to thank You for all the things you have given and shown me…Please help me to become a better person. I really want to be able to know You better and show Your love. Also, just be with me through my finals – especially chemistry! Also guide me through my college life and this summer. Thank You for everything.*
>
> *I love You!*
>
> *Beth*

It's a pretty simple letter, but writing letters like this over the past 25 years has helped me get to know God better, it's a great way to write down your prayers for others, and when you read your journal you will be really happy to see how well you are getting to know the Lord.

MY PERSONAL WALK WITH GOD
Pages You Can Personalize!

Special People In My Life - I Can Pray For Each Of These People

You might need your parents to help you with this!

My Parents and/or Step Parents:

Name/Birthdate:_____

Name/Birthdate:_____

Name/Birthdate:_____

Name/Birthdate:_____

My Brothers and Sisters:

Name/Birthdate:_____

Name/Birhdate:_____

Name/Birthdate:_____

Name/Birthdate:_____

My Pets:

Type of Animal/Name/Birthdate:_____

Type of Animal/Name/Birthdate:_____

39

My Grandparents:

Name/Birthdate:_____

Name/Birthdate:_____

Name/Birthdate:_____

Name/Birthdate:_____

My Friends:

Name/Birthdate:_____

Name/Birthdate:_____

Name/Birthdate:_____

Name/Birthdate:_____

My Pastors & Children's Church Teachers:

Name/Birthdate:_____

Name/Birthdate:_____

Name/Birthdate:_____

Name/Birthdate:_____

My School Teachers:

Name/Birthdate:_____

Name/Birthdate:_____

Name/Birthdate:_____

Name/Birthdate:_____

CHAPTER 5
Hearing God's Voice
"How To Read Your Bible"

How does God talk to you? Will you hear his voice out of heaven? Probably not! God talks to His children through the Bible. God's Word, the Bible, is God's personal love letter to you. As you read the Bible, you will sense that God Himself is whispering in your spiritual ear. The Bible is unlike any other book because it is alive and full of life and power.

 MY STORY: *I remember when I first started reading the Bible. The Bible was different than any other book I had read. It seemed to be alive! It wasn't a boring schoolbook or just facts on a page; it seemed like God was sitting on my shoulder and talking to my heart as I read the Bible!*

Just like you eat food every day for your body to grow strong, you need to eat spiritual food every day, too. When you read your Bible it's just like eating spiritual food for your spirit to grow strong. Since the Bible will give you spiritual food, strength, light and power, the devil will do anything he can to distract you from reading it. Your Bible will teach you everything you need to know about how to walk in God's blessings in this life. It is no wonder Satan fights so hard to keep you from reading it! If you will read your Bible every day, God will show you many things about His love and all that He has planned for your life.

Let's look at this exciting Book!

A. WHO WROTE THE BIBLE?

1. 2 Timothy 3:16

   Who inspired men to write all that is in the Bible?_____

2. John 5:39

   Jesus told us what the main theme of the Bible is.

   Who do the Scriptures tell us about?

   _____

B.   HOW LONG WILL GOD'S WORD BE TRUE?

1.   Matthew 24:35

      How long will God's Words last?_____

2.   1 Peter 1:25

      How long will God's Word last?_____

3.   Isaiah 40:8

      The flowers and grass will turn brown and wither away, but what will God's Word do?

      _____

THE BIBLE IS A SUPERNATURAL BOOK: Did you know the Bible is unlike any other Book in history? It is alive! The Bible was written by forty different men who had different careers. Some were fisherman, some were farmers, some were doctors, some were kings and some were preachers – God used forty different people that had different kinds of jobs to write His Words. It took 1500 years to write the Bible. God used people from different generations to write His Words! It was written in three different languages – Hebrew, Aramaic and Greek. Today, we read our whole Bible in English, but it was originally written in these three languages. The Bible has one central theme – Jesus Christ is the star of every part of the Bible. It is obvious that there was really One Supreme Author – God, the Holy Spirit, was in charge of writing the Bible!

C.   HOW DOES GOD'S WORD HELP US?

1.   2 Timothy 3:16,17

      God's Word is useful to help us know what is _____

      What does God's Word tell us about our lives?_____

2.   Hebrews 4:12

      How sharp is God's Word?_____

What does it do in our hearts?_____

3.   Psalm 119:11, 105

If we hide God's Word in our hearts, how does that help us?_____

How does God's Word help us walk in His paths?_____

4.   Psalm 119:103

What does God's Word taste like to our hearts?_____

5.   Matthew 4:4

What do we need to eat if we want to have a strong life with God?_____

6.   Luke 8:4-15

This is the story of the "sower and the seed". Jesus is showing us how God's Word is like a seed and our hearts are like the ground. He describes four different types of soil or hearts. Can you describe what happened to the seed of God's Word that was planted in these four hearts?

The Hard Path:_____

The Rocky Soil:_____

The Thorny Soil:_____

The Good Soil:_____

D.   WHAT ARE WE SUPPOSED TO DO WITH GOD'S WORD?

1.   Colossians 3:16

Where is God's Word supposed to live?_____

It is our job to read the Bible so that God's Word fills our heart fully!

2.   2 Timothy 2:15

As we grow and learn God's Word, what does God want us to be able to do?_____

3.   Joshua 1:8

How often are we to study and think about God's Word in our lives?_____

When we know God's Word and obey it, what does He promise?_____

4.   James 1:21-25

After we hear God's message, what are we to do with it?_____

What happens if we hear God's Word, but we do not obey it?_____

What happens if we hear God's Word, and we do obey it?_____

E.   WHO HELPS US UNDERSTAND THE WORD?

Your parents, pastor, Sunday school teachers or other Christians may help teach you the Bible, but the best Teacher of all is the Holy Spirit. He will speak directly to your heart as you read the Bible. Let's look at this.

John 14:23-26

Who will teach us and remind us of everything Jesus tells us in the Word?_____

F.   JUST DO IT - TAKE ACTION

Now it's time to just do it! Let's take action on what we have studied. Look up this passage.

2 Timothy 3:14-15

Timothy was a young man when the Apostle Paul wrote him the letters of 1 Timothy and 2 Timothy. Notice what Paul said about Timothy in verse 15.

When was Timothy taught the Scriptures; the Bible?_____

What did it do for him?_____

Why not decide right now that you will spend the first 5-10 minutes of the day reading your Bible. Or maybe you can spend the last 5-10 minutes of the day, right before you go to sleep, reading your Bible. Talk to your parents to develop a plan for your Bible reading and learning. Be sure to include things like going to church regularly, maybe listening to the Bible on cassette tape or CD, listening to other teaching tapes and reading books and autobiographies that will boost your faith.

Kids can learn, know and grow from reading the Bible. God will talk to you through His Word and lead you in the way He has for you. If you will put God's Word first in your life – if you will expect God to speak to your heart and if you will obey what He tells you – you will live a life blessed by God!

I want to challenge you to read through the entire Bible, at least once, by the time you graduate from high school. Here are some ideas on how you can have fun reading your Bible. Why don't you pick one and get started!

1. Read Proverbs each month - by reading just 1 chapter in Proverbs each day!

2. Read Psalms each month - by reading just 5 Psalms each day!

3. Read the "Go Eat Pop Corn" books - by reading Galatians, Ephesians, Philippians and Colossians.

4. Read the Old & New Testaments each day - by reading just 1 Chapter in the Old Testament and 1 chapter in the New Testament each day.

5. Read the Gospel of Matthew in a week - by reading just 4 chapters each day!

6. Read the Book of Acts in a week - by reading just 4 chapters each day.

7. Read the Gospel of John and 1st, 2nd, and 3rd John in 1 week - by reading just 4 chapters each day.

8. EXTREME CHRISTIANS: Read the entire New Testament in 26 days - by reading just 10 chapters each day! Wow!!!

MY PERSONAL WALK WITH GOD
Pages You Can Personalize!

Fun Bible Thoughts

If you could choose any animal from the Bible to have for a pet, which one would it be? What would you name it?

Next to Jesus, who is your favorite person in the Bible?

If Jesus came to your house for dinner, what would you want Him to tell you?

Of all the names in the Bible, which one would you want?

Circle the Bible character or Bible family you would like to live with if you could go back in time.

Abraham and Sarah	Joseph
Noah's Family	Ruth & Naomi
Moses Family	Esther
Gideon	Joshua
Samson	Mary & Joseph
David's Family	Nicodemus
Daniel	John the Baptist
Peter	Timothy
Paul	John the Apostle

CHAPTER 6

OBEYING GOD
"HOW TO HAVE GOD'S BEST"

God wants your life to be blessed. Did you know there is a life God blesses? It's the person who believes and trusts in the Lord and then receives His love and goodness and obeys what He tells them. Sure, you may face trials and tests at times, but if you'll listen to the Lord and follow Him and His Word, in the end you will be a blessed kid. He has promised us that He will help us through any difficulty and that He will bless our lives as we obey Him and follow His directions.

A. WHY SHOULD WE OBEY GOD AND FOLLOW HIM?

    1.   1 John 4:8

        What does this verse tell us about God – God is_____

        Since God is love – it is easy to obey Him! Because God loves us, we want to obey Him. We don't obey Him to get Him to love us. He calls us His "beloved" and He loves us more than anyone and wants the very best for us.

    2.   John 14:15

        How do we show God that we love Him?_____

    3.   John 14:21,23,24

        According to these verses, who really loves God?_____

        If a person says he loves God, but doesn't obey God, what do you think that means?

        _____

B. WHAT DOES GOD WANT US TO OBEY?

    1.   God Wants Us To Love

a. John 13:34,35

Who are we supposed to love?_____

What does our love prove?_____

b. Matthew 22:36-40

What is the most important command God gave us?_____

c. Romans 13:10

If we love others, what will we never do?_____

d. John 15:12-17

What is the greatest way to show others you love them?_____

What do you think that means in every day life?_____

D. WHAT HAPPENS WHEN WE OBEY GOD?

1. Luke 6:46-49
Read the story and place an "x" in the column that answers the question.

	Obedient	Disobedient
Who heard what Jesus said?		
Who obeyed God's Words?		
Who faced a storm?		
Whose house fell?		
Whose house stood firm?		

Keep in mind, we obey God from a position of being loved, not from a fearful position. He wants our lives to be strong, blessed and filled with His goodness that's why He speaks His wisdom to us through His Word.

E.   OBEY YOUR PARENTS

When you are a child, God wants you to obey your parents. God gave you parents to love you, nourish you and protect you. It's important that you obey God by obeying your parents. Let's look at this.

1.   Ephesians 6:1-3

Children, what does God want you to do?_____

Why?_____

What two things has God promised to those children who obey and honor their parents?

_____

_____

Would you like to live a long life?_____

Would you like a life of blessing?_____

2.   Luke 2:41-52

In verse 51, what did Jesus do?_____

3.   Proverbs 1:8-9

Why should we listen to and obey our mom and dad?_____

50

F.   OBEY GOD IN THESE AREAS

1.   Pick the Right Kind of Friends

Did you know that God is interested in the people you choose as friends? God wants you to love everyone, but He doesn't want you to be friends with just anyone.

FRIENDS: God is concerned about whom you choose for a friend and He has told us to choose friends that love Him. That's because He wants our lives to be blessed. Some kids don't love God. Some kids like to rebel against their parents. Some kids like to swear, or steal, or look at naughty things on videos, in magazines or on the internet. Some kids like music that has bad lyrics and they don't like to listen to Christian music at all. There are some kids that like to smoke cigarettes or joints, and some like to drink beer and take drugs. Maybe there are some kids in your neighborhood or at school that you think are nice kids, but sometimes they do some of the things we mentioned. What should you do? Ignore them? Be mean to them? No! You should pray for them because maybe they haven't heard about Jesus yet. In the meantime, look for other friends who share your love for the Lord.

1 Corinthians 15:33

How would you describe people that are "bad company"?_____

2.   Keep Your Heart Pure

Proverbs 4:22

What does God want us to do with our hearts?_____

Why is it important to keep a pure heart in God's sight?_____

3.   Speak Good Words

Ephesians 4:29

What kind of words did God say we shouldn't use?_____

What kind of words does God want us to use?_____

G. JUST DO IT - TAKE ACTION

Now it's time to just do it! Let's take action on what we have studied. I want to encourage you to be quick to obey God's Word by loving God and loving others and by obeying your parents. If you will learn this as a child, you will save yourself from difficulties later in life and you will enjoy a peaceful heart and God's blessings in your life.

What are some ways you can be more obedient to your parents?_____

_____

I know that you will make a good decision to do your best to obey God. However, sometimes we make mistakes. Can you think of areas where you have been disobedient? In our next chapter, we'll discuss how to obtain God's forgiveness.

Let's take a few minutes to look up this prayer in Colossians 1:9-10 and let's pray it for ourselves right now!

Dear Father,

I pray and ask You to fill me with the knowledge of Your will. Give me spiritual wisdom and understanding. I pray that I may live a life pleasing to You in every way. I pray I bear fruit in every good work and that I grow in my knowledge of You. In Jesus' Name. Amen.

MY PERSONAL WALK WITH GOD
Pages You Can Personalize!

I love God...
Draw a picture of
you worshiping the Lord

I love people...
Draw a picture of
you   showing love to others

...I want to go to church...
Draw of picture of your church

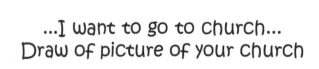

CHAPTER 7
Being Forgiven
"How To Experience God's Love & Forgiveness"

Have you ever blown it? Messed up? Disobeyed? Made a mistake? We all have. When we blow it, mess up, or make a mistake – we have sinned. If we are honest, our hearts begin to condemn us and we feel guilty. Sometimes, we cover our guilty feelings up with anger, frustration and depression. Enough of these negative feelings and we can get to the point that we actually feel sick. If we don't deal with the guilt we experience when we sin, we will feel far away from God.

 MY STORY: *I remember when I was in second grade I messed up big time! I had always had an open, honest relationship with my parents and I had always tried to be a good girl. I did two really bad things in second grade. First, my teacher caught me and my friends writing naughty notes back and forth to each other. We were making up mean poems about people and our teacher snatched our notes from us. I was horrified! Fortunately, one of the notes we wrote my teacher didn't snatch and I hid it in my desk, way back in the corner. I felt so guilty! My conscience really bothered me. I was so afraid that my teacher would tell my parents about these bad notes. I was afraid that someone would search my desk and find the note I had hidden. I never told my parents about the notes. My teacher never told my parents about the notes. I never asked God to forgive me, until two years later!! I was then in fourth grade, and one night the guilt feelings were so heavy on me as I thought about those notes. I faked like I had a headache and began to cry. My parents asked me what was wrong and I told them I had a really bad headache, but they could tell by the way I was acting that it really wasn't a headache, and they began to ask me what was really wrong. Finally, I told them that I just felt so guilty and bad about these notes that I had written when I was in second grade and that I had not told them about it. Guess what they said? They said they loved me and told me how proud of me they were for being honest. They forgave me and my heart felt so much better! All the guilt feelings were gone and I was forgiven.*

 MY STORY: *Another dumb thing I did in second grade was that I was mean to a girl named Sally. Everyone picked on Sally and I thought I should pick on her, too. One day right before school, I was inside the school building and I saw Sally walking up to the doors. I decided that I would hold the doors shut so that she couldn't get inside the building. I just laughed at her and held the doors shut. I was being so mean. Just when the bell rang, I let go of the doors, turned to run to class and guess who I ran into? The principal! I ran right into his legs! I was busted! Guess who got to laugh now? Sally! I was caught red handed. I was so scared of our principal that I just shook and wet my pants right in school! Can you imagine how embarrassing that was? I didn't look too cool then! I was humbled right then and I learned a good lesson about doing the right thing! I was never mean to Sally again!*

Here's a story that will help us to understand how much God loves us and how much He wants to help us when we blow it!

WHAT WOULD YOU DO? Suppose you were riding your bike or your skateboard or your scooter in your driveway one sunny day. When your mom called you into the house for dinner, you zoomed into the garage on your bike, skateboard or scooter, and you accidentally ran right into your dad's car! What if your bike pedal scraped the side of your dad's car and left a big scratch and a small dent? Or...what if you did some skateboard trick and your skateboard kicked up and the wheels and trucks of the board scraped your dad's car and damaged it? Or...what if it was your scooter handle bars that scraped the side of your dad's car? After you hit the car, you immediately check to see what kind of damage you have done. When you see the damage you don't know what to do. You are wrestling with the question, "Should I tell dad?" You decide that you aren't going to say anything about it to your dad. If you don't tell your dad what you did, maybe your dad will assume that something else hit his car. Maybe he'll think the door of another car scratched his car while he was parked at work or something like that. Besides, if you did tell your dad, maybe you would get in trouble, be grounded or lose the privilege of using your bike, skateboard or scooter for a while. What you don't know is that your dad saw the whole thing. He opened the garage door to take out the trash and he watched you slide right into his car. He saw you check the damage – he saw it all! At dinner, your dad is waiting for you to tell him what happened. When you don't say anything, how do you think that affects your relationship with him?

How do you think the dad feels?_____

Do you think the father and the child are feeling close to one another right now?_____

What should the kid do if he wants to feel close to his father again?_____

Do you think the father still loves his child?_____

Our relationship with our Heavenly Father is similar to our relationship with our earthly fathers. Our heavenly Father knows everything we think and He sees everything we do. God loves us and because of Jesus death on the cross, He's forgiven our sins -- He wants us to be honest with Him about our mistakes so He can cleanse the guilty we feel in our conscience and we can stay close to Him.

What does God want us to do when we mess up, do mean things or disobey Him?_____

Will God help us to experience His love and forgiveness?_____

A. WHAT IS SIN?

Sin is when we disobey God or we disobey our parents and even our own hearts. These verses tell us how God defines sin.

1.   James 4:17

        What is a sin?_____

2.   Romans 14:23

        If you do anything you think is not right, you are_____

B. WHO SINS?

1.   Romans 3:23

        Who has sinned?_____

2.   1 John 1:8,10

        If we say we have not sinned, what are we doing?_____

        If we claim we have not sinned, what are we calling God?_____

C. GOD TELLS US NOT TO SIN

1.   1 Corinthians 15:34

        God wants us to stop_____

2.   James 1:13-16

        Who never tempts us to sin?_____

        Where does temptation come from?_____

TEMPTATION: It is important to remember that temptation is not sin. To be tempted is normal for a Christian. Jesus was tempted by the devil, and yet He never sinned. When you are tempted, don't let the enemy make you feel as if you have already sinned. Resist the temptation and you will not sin. Someone once said, you can't stop a bird from flying over your head, but you can stop it from building a nest in your hair. Temptation is like that bird flying overhead. When you resist the temptation it can't build nest in your hair!

D. HOW CAN WE RESIST THE TEMPTATION TO SIN?

1 Corinthians 10:13

Are the temptations you face different than what others face?_____

What will God do for you when you are tempted?_____

E. WHAT DO WE DO IF WE SIN?

Always remember that God loves you and He is always there for you to turn to and talk to when you make a mistake or mess up. Don't ever run from Him, but run to Him with your problems. He is the one who has all the answers and who will give you forgiveness.

1 John 1:9

This verse has been called the Christian's "bar of soap".

What are we supposed to do when we sin?_____

When we confess our sins to God – that means we tell God the sin or sins we have done. Because of Jesus, when we received Him as our Lord all of our sins were forgiven, but when we mess up, we feel guilt in our conscience. That's why, when we make a mistake, we can run right to God and confess our sins to Him. We let Him know that we agree with Him that what we did or failed to do was a sin. Through His forgiveness, He instantly cleanses our guilty conscience from all unrighteousness.

After we confess our sins, what will God do?_____

What does God cleanse us from?_____

F. WHERE DOES SIN GO?

1. Hebrews 8:12 and Hebrews 10:17

    The Lord will not_____ our sins.

2. Micah 7:19

    Because Jesus took our sins on the cross, God throws our sins into_____

G. A STORY OF A SINFUL SON AND A FORGIVING FATHER

Luke 15:11-32

Jesus told us the story of a boy who left home and went into the world to party, waste his money and live an ungodly life. He no longer wanted to be with his father, but chose to do things he knew were not right. He thought it would be fun to sin. After a while he found out that it wasn't fun to sin...he was broke, he had to eat the food that pigs eat, he didn't have any real friends and he was lonely. He wanted to go back home, but he didn't know what his father would think. He decided to go home and confess his sins to his father. When he arrived home, he told his dad that he had sinned and he was very sorry. Let's look at this story.

In verse 21, what did the son tell his father he'd done?_____

In verse 20, was the father glad that his son had come home?_____

What did the father do when he saw his son?_____

In verses 22-24, was the son treated like a sinner, a son or a servant?_____

Just think, that's how your Heavenly Father feels about you -- even when you sin. Always remember to run quickly to the Lord, tell him you are sorry, and then thank Him for forgiving you. Remember that you are still a special son or daughter that He loves very much.

G. JUST DO IT - TAKE ACTION

Now it's time to just do it! Let's take action on what we have studied. It's so important to keep an honest and pure heart before God. If you will confess your sins to Him when you blow it, you will enjoy a loving friendship with the Lord.

Maybe it would be helpful for you to take a moment to do just what 1 John 1:9 tells us to do.

- On a piece of paper, why don't you write down any sins that you have done that you have not already confessed to the Lord.

- Once you've written them down, look up 1 John 1:9 and read it out loud.

- After you have read it, write "1 John 1:9" in big letters across that piece of paper.

- Now say, "Because of Jesus, all of these sins are forgiven, and I am cleansed from the guilt of all wrong doing."

- Now, tear that piece of paper up into little, tiny pieces and throw those pieces away, never to be remembered!

This is exactly what God did with our sin when Jesus went to the cross. When we received Jesus as our Lord, He made us as righteous as God Himself and because of that, when we make a mistake and confess it to Him, He instantly cleanses our guilty conscience.

MY PERSONAL WALK WITH GOD
Pages You Can Personalize!

10 Things I am Really Thankful For:

Did you know that you can obey God by giving thanks?
That's what He told us to do in 1 Thessalonians 5:18.

Make a list of 10 things that you are thankful for...
then why don't you personally tell the Lord "thank you" for each of those things!

1.

2.

3.

4.

5.

6.

7.

8.

9.

10.

CHAPTER 8
Being Filled With The Holy Spirit
"How To Flow With The Spirit"

Do you play sports? Have you watched athletes on television? Have you ever watched the Olympics? Have you noticed that when athletes are working really hard they sweat? They need to drink lots of water if they are going to be full of energy and strength in competition. Did you know this is true for Christians? We are like athletes for God! We are running in the Christian race! Every day we are training as we get to know God, as we pray to God, as we love people and then when we are running to tell as many people as we can about how they can know Jesus and go to heaven. It is so exciting to be an athlete for God! Sometimes we need a big drink of God's water so that we can be full of God's energy and strength. When we are filled with the Holy Spirit, it's like God is filling us up with His water so that we can run our race for Him full of power, energy and strength!

Do you remember when we talked about the Trinity or Godhead – God the Father, Jesus the Son and the Holy Spirit? Once we've asked Jesus into our hearts to be our Lord, the Bible calls us Christians or believers. We now have a Heavenly Father and Jesus as our friend. But more exciting things are in store for us. We have the opportunity to receive more of God in our lives. We can ask our Father and Jesus to fill us with His Holy Spirit. Would you like to be filled up with more of God? In some places in the Bible this is called being "filled with the Holy Spirit", "receiving the Holy Spirit" or "being baptized in the Holy Spirit".

Let's look in our Bibles to find out more.

A. GOD WANTS YOU TO BE FULL OF HIS POWER

Acts 1:8

When the Holy Spirit fills you, what happens?_____

Why does God fill you with His power?_____

Have you ever told other people about Jesus?_____

Would you like God to give you power so that you can tell people about Jesus?_____

Someone once described "being filled with the Spirit" and the power that can come from our lives as being like taking a Coke can and shaking it up...and then opening the lid! Because the can is "full of Coke", Coke sprays all over the place! Jesus wants to "spray" from your life all over people, and He does this when you are filled with the Spirit!

B.   GOD HAS A GIFT FOR YOU

1.   Acts 2:38-39

Peter called the Holy Spirit a_____

Do you like gifts?_____

Who did Peter say this promised gift was for?_____

Does that include you?_____

Do you think God gives good gifts?_____

Aren't you glad that God said this gift was for children? _____

2.   Acts 1:4-5

What did Jesus tell His disciples they would be baptized with?_____

3.   Acts 2:4

When Jesus gave His disciples the gift of the Holy Spirit, what happened?_____

4.   Ephesians 5:18-20

What does God want His children to be filled with?_____

What does God not want His children to do?_____

When we are filled with the Spirit, what will we enjoy doing?_____

C. WHO RECEIVED THIS GIFT IN THE BIBLE?

1. Matthew 3:16

   The Holy Spirit _____ on Jesus.

2. Acts 2:4

   Everyone present was_____ with the Spirit.

3. Acts 8:17

   These believers_____ the Holy Spirit.

4. Acts 9:17

   Brother Saul (the Apostle Paul) was_____ with the Holy Spirit.

5. Acts 10:47

   The Holy Spirit _____ on everyone who heard and received the message.

6. Acts 19:6

   When Paul laid hands on these disciples, the Holy Spirit_____ them.

D. YOU CAN RECEIVE GOD'S GIFT

1. James 1:17

   God gives us good and perfect gifts. God's gifts are described as:

   Whatever is _____ and _____ comes from God above.

2. Luke 11:9-13

   How do we obtain gifts from God?_____

List what the son did not expect to get when he asked his father for…

Bread – he did not expect_____

Fish – he did not expect_____

Egg – he did not expect_____

What will your Heavenly Father give you if you ask for the Holy Spirit?_____

E.   YOU WILL RECEIVE A SPECIAL LANGUAGE FROM GOD

Did you know that as a Christian you are like a special agent for God? You are on a mission and God gives you His energy and power to do your mission. Not only that, He gives you a special code language that only He understands! The Bible calls this speaking in tongues or speaking in the Spirit.

Have you ever wanted to have a secret language that you and your friends could use to talk to each other? When I was a kid, my sisters and I made up a special code language that no one but us could understand. It was called "jibberish". We could talk in complete sentences and our friends and even our parents couldn't figure out what we were saying! We had a lot of fun using this language to frustrate my mother!

Guess what? God wants you to have a special language so that you can talk and pray things to Him that the devil can't understand! You are God's secret agent and He has a special language just for you.

1.   Acts 2:4

What could these believers do when they were filled with the Holy Spirit?_____

2.   Acts 10:45-46

When the Gentile believers were filled with the Spirit, what did they do?_____

3.   Acts 19:6

When the Holy Spirit filled these believers, what happened?_____

F. HOW TO USE YOUR SPECIAL LANGUAGE

1. 1 Corinthians 14:2

    Who are you talking to when you speak in tongues?_____

2. 1 Corinthians 14:4

    What happens to a person who speaks in tongues?_____

    Have you ever seen your parents charge the battery to the car? Or have you ever charged rechargeable batteries at home? As long as the batteries are plugged into the battery charger, they will be revived with power and energy! This is the same thing that happens to us when we pray or speak in tongues to God. When we use our secret language, it is like we are plugged into God's battery charger and we get filled with His power and energy.

3. 1 Corinthians 14:18

    What did the Apostle Paul say he did more than anyone?_____

4. 1 Corinthians 14:15

    What two things did Paul say he could do in the Spirit?

    _____

    _____

G. JUST DO IT - TAKE ACTION

Now it's time to just do it! Let's take action on what we have studied. Would you like to be filled with the Spirit? Would you like more of God's energy to tell others of Jesus? Would you like to have a supernatural code language that you can speak to God?

It's really simple to be filled with the Spirit.

1. First, you must already be a born-again Christian.

2.   Second, you let God know that you are sorry for any sins you have committed and you let Him know you want every one of His gifts in your life.

3.   Third, you must simply ask God the Father to fill you with His Spirit. You can pray a prayer like this:

Dear Heavenly Father, I ask you in Jesus' Name to fill me with the Holy Spirit. I thank You for Your good gift of the Holy Spirit and I want to be full of Your power and energy so that I can tell everyone about Jesus. I also want to know You better and I want to be able to talk to You from my heart of hearts in the special language of speaking in tongues. Father, I receive Your gift of the Holy Spirit right now. Thank You – in Jesus' Name I pray. Amen.

4.   Fourth, now that you have received God's gift, tell Him thank You. Take a moment to praise Him for everything He is doing and is going to do in your life.

5.   Fifth, from your heart you begin to speak in your secret language to your Heavenly Father.

I want to encourage you to talk to your parents or your Pastor or Sunday School teacher about this more. It may be helpful to have them pray with you and coach you more on how you can be filled continually with the Spirit.

MY PERSONAL WALK WITH GOD
Pages You Can Personalize!

I want to be filled with the Spirit so that I can have power to...

Be a witness...
draw a picture of you preaching!

Pray with power...
draw a picture of God in heaven listening to your prayers!

Understand the Bible...
draw a picture of a lightbulb in your head!

Speak to God in a language I don't know...
draw a picture of you praying in your prayer language!

CHAPTER 9
Being Strong In Faith
"How To Please God"

God wants you to be a champion for Him! Did you know that anyone in the Bible who was a champion for God was a person with strong faith? People with strong faith see God do awesome things in their lives. God has already given you some faith. You used your faith to believe in Him, didn't you? He has given you a portion of faith. Now it's up to you to add to your faith. It's up to you to grow and develop more faith. God wants you to be a person of great faith!

FAITH MUSCLES: Think of it this way. God has given you muscles, hasn't He? You have biceps, triceps and all kinds of other muscles. I know kids like to tighten their tummys to see if they can show off a six-pack of muscles! They like to pump up their arm muscles to see who has bigger biceps! Your whole body is filled with muscles. You got those muscles when you were born, right? What you do with those muscles is up to you. You can sit on the couch and play video games your whole life and end up being an 80-pound weakling r you can become the strongest kid in the neighborhood by developing your muscles. If you do a few sit ups and push ups, or if you play soccer or basketball or gymnastics, or if you get involved in active sports like snowboarding or skateboarding, you will develop big muscles. These various activities will help you develop bigger, stronger muscles. If you want really, really big strong muscles, then you will have to be even more dedicated and devoted to exercising and working out than the average kid, right? Think of the weight lifters you see on television. Have you ever seen the power lifters? The ironman? Have you ever seen those muscled body builders up close? The muscles on the men and women who lift weights every day are so big and strong. Those muscles didn't grow by accident; muscular people have to be very disciplined and dedicated to growing their muscles every day.

Did you know it's the same way with our faith? When you became a born-again Christian, God gave you "faith muscles". You have faith for salvation. You have faith for your prayers to be answered. You have faith for lots of things, but at first your faith is small and weak. What you do with your faith muscles is up to you. You can sit in front of the TV, play video games and movies all day or you can spend all your time listening to music videos and playing on the Internet and you'll end up being a weak little baby Christian. People with weak faith muscles are weak spiritually and often these kind of people are afraid, or sad, or angry, or mean, or they don't know how to control their mouths. Many times, people with weak faith muscles don't know that they can develop their faith muscles to replace their fears with peace, to replace their sadness with joy and laughter, to replace their anger with kindness, to replace their mean spirit with God's love and to replace a mouthy mouth with words that will bless them and other people. Do you want to be a kid with weak faith muscles? I don't believe you do! Let's look at how we can have strong faith muscles. How would you like to be a "strong man" spiritually? You can become the strongest spiritual kid in your church or school by developing your faith muscles. How? You'll have to lift spiritual weights each day! If you'll take time each day to talk to God, to read your Bible or listen to God's Word, that is just like lifting spiritual weights and it will help you to develop bigger, stronger faith muscles.

Jesus said that we could have faith muscles so strong that we could move mountains! Have you ever faced a mountain or difficulty in your life that you feel like you couldn't fix or change? With mountain-moving faith things can change in your life! If you want to have the kind of faith that Jesus tells us to have, if you want mountain-moving faith, then you will have to be more committed and dedicated to praying to God and reading your Bible than the average kid. When you have giant faith muscles nothing is impossible. Jesus said nothing is impossible for those who believe – for those who have muscles of faith!

Let's look at this.

A.   WHAT IS FAITH?

Do you know what faith is? It's really simple. Faith is believing God's Word! When we believe God and His Word, we have faith. When we trust God and His Word, we have faith.

1.   Hebrews 11:1,6

What is faith?_____

Can you please God without faith?_____

What does God do for those who sincerely seek Him?_____

To have faith in God means to have faith in His Word. God wants us to believe everything in His Word. We started our walk of faith when we asked Jesus to come into our hearts. We didn't see Jesus, or feel Jesus, or taste Jesus, or touch Jesus, or smell Jesus – but we knew in our hearts that He was real because we believed God's Word and we invited Him into our lives – right? That is faith!

2.   Hebrews 11:4-30

This is called "God's Hall of Faith"! If you are an outstanding baseball player or football player or basketball player, you might have a chance to someday be in the Hall of Fame, but if you are a person of faith, you can be in God's Hall of Faith! These people used their faith to do mighty things for God. List the name of each person mentioned in the verse:

Verse 4_____

Verse 5_____

Verse 7_____

Verse 8_____

Verse 11_____

Verse 20_____

Verse 21_____

Verse 22_____

Verse 23 _____

Verse 24_____

Verse 29_____

Verse 31_____

Verse 32-33_____

B. WIMPY FAITH OR STRONG FAITH?

Look up these verses and see if we are learning about wimpy faith or strong faith. Write the word "wimpy" or "strong" next to the verse.

1.   Matthew 6:30_____

2.   Matthew 8:10 (Luke 7:9)_____

3.   Matthew 8:26_____

4.   Matthew 14:31_____

5.   Matthew 15:28_____

6.   Matthew 16:8_____

7.   Romans 4:19_____

8.   Romans 4:20_____

C. GROWING STRONGER FAITH MUSCLES

1.   2 Corinthians 10:15

        What does the Apostle Paul hope our faith will do?_____

2.   Romans 10:17

        Faith comes when we do what?_____

        More faith comes to us when we read and think about God's Word.

D. HOW TO USE YOUR FAITH

Our faith muscles need to be used! The way you begin using your faith muscles is by doing something! The way you use the muscles in your body is by doing something! When you exercise, your muscles are used. One primary way we exercise our faith muscles is by using our mouth to agree with God's Word. When we say the same thing with our mouths that God's Word says and that we believe in our hearts, we are using our faith. When our heart and our mouth agree, our faith is in action!

Our faith muscle is used when we do this two-part equation.

Believing God's Word in our hearts + Saying God's Word with our mouth = Faith

✝ **FAITH IN ACTION:** For example, let's say you read Psalm 91 about God's protection. If you believe it, what should you do with your mouth? If we believe in our hearts God's Word in Psalm 91, that God will protect us and then we say with our mouths, "I am so scared and afraid of everything," what happens? We are believing one thing, but saying something different and our faith won't work! We have a faith muscle, but it is not being used properly and God cannot answer our faith because it is confused. On one hand we say we believe God will protect us, and then with our mouth we say how scared we are. If we really believed God would protect us, what kind of words would we say?

✝ **FAITH IN ACTION:** Take another example, the story of Daniel. Daniel was a young man who had great faith! He put God first and obeyed God more than anyone else and God blessed him immensely! If you put God first in your life and heart, then you can use your faith to believe God's Word in Daniel 1:17-20 will work for you too. If you believe, according to Daniel 1:17-20, that God will help you with your learning, understanding and schoolwork, but say with your mouth, "I am so stupid and confused," what will happen? God won't be able to answer your faith because you have a faith muscle, but it is not being used properly and God cannot answer our faith because it is confused. On one hand, we say we believe God will help us with our schoolwork and then with our mouth we say how stupid and confused we are. If we really believed God would help us with our schoolwork, what kind of words would we say?

Can you see how important it is to say words that agree with God's Words? To say words that you believe in your heart?

1.   2 Corinthians 4:13

        I believed and therefore I _____

2.   Romans 10:8-10

If you_____ that Jesus is Lord

If you_____ that God raised Him from the dead

You will_____

3.   Mark 11:22-23

God wants us to develop mountain-moving faith! Mountains can represent any difficulty in your life. Is there an obstacle in your life? Is something really bothering you and trying to get you down? You need to use your mountain-moving faith!

In verse 22, what did Jesus tell us to have?_____

In verse 23, do we pray to the mountain?_____

In verse 23, do we pray to God about the mountain?_____

In verse 23, do we speak to the mountain?_____

What will obey our command?_____

When we speak words of faith, what are we to have in our hearts?_____

E.   JUST DO IT – TAKE ACTION

Now it's time to just do it! Let's take action on what we have studied. Do you want to be one of God's super strong faith muscle kids? How are you going to develop your faith muscles? It will take more commitment than other kids are willing to give. You don't want to be a weak Christian, do you? Are you willing to discipline yourself to read God's Word every day? Are you willing to give up some of your time playing video games to read God's Word? Are you willing to give up some of your play time to put God's Word first? Are you willing to get your mouth in agreement with God's Word -- even when you don't feel like it? Are you willing to give up some of the negative words you are in the habit of saying and start saying words that agree with God's Word? If you will, you will see God's blessing in your life!

Your heart will get so full of God's Word that as you speak God's Word out, you will release a powerful force called faith. Mountains will move in your life and your name can be written in God's Hall of Faith.

YOUR PERSONAL PLAN: What is your plan for developing your faith muscles?

I want to read my Bible for _____ minutes each day.

I want to read my Bible during this time _____ each day.

I would suggest that you talk to your parents about getting the audio version of the New Testament so you can play it each night before you go to bed. Let God's Word begin to fill your heart and watch those faith muscles grow!

MY PERSONAL WALK WITH GOD
Pages You Can Personalize!

<u>Bible Trivia</u>

What's the first word in the Bible?

What's the last word in the Bible?

Who's the oldest person in the Bible?

How many times did Jesus say, "Fear Not"?

What is the shortest verse in the Bible?

Name the 12 disciples.

Name or sing all the books of the Bible.

What is the last book in the Old Testament?

Who wrote Genesis?

Name the four Gospels.

<u>Bible Jokes</u>

Where did they play baseball in the Bible?

Where does it say the church drove a Honda?

Answers:
In Genesis it says - in the beginning (big inning)
In Acts - it says they were all in one Accord

CHAPTER 10
Living Life to the Max
"How to be Blessed"

God wants your life blessed. Did you know that? He really does. There is a life that God blesses. There is also a life that God cannot bless. We see examples in the Bible of people who believed God, received His promises, obeyed what He told them and they were so blessed by the Lord that they lived lives with a happy heart. They lived long lives, they were strong and healthy, they had lots of great friends, they were rich, they were influential, and they were mightily used by God. It doesn't mean they didn't have trials and challenges, they did. But, with God's help they were able to overcome. Is that the kind of life you would like? There were others who always had bad attitudes, doubted everything and lived lives of rebellion that didn't please the Lord. They died early, were sick and weak, were unhappy and depressed -- and they lived sad, boring, empty lives. What kind of life do you want? What kind of life does God really want you to have?

A.   THE LIFE GOD WANTS YOU TO HAVE

1.   John 10:10

What does Jesus want us to have?_____

What does the thief (the devil) want us to have?_____

2.   Psalm 103:1-5

What does God want us to never forget?_____

What does God do to all of our sins?_____

What does God do to all of our diseases?_____

3.   3 John 2

What did the Apostle John pray for his friends?_____

4.   Deuteronomy 28:1-14

In verses 1-2, what will God do in our lives if we fully obey Him?_____

In verses 3-14, list all the blessings God has promised us:

_____

_____

5.   Deuteronomy 30:15,19-20

God is giving us a choice. What are our choices?

_____   _____

What does God want us to choose?_____

If we choose to love the Lord our God and to obey His Word, what does He promise?

_____

Did you know that God wants you to be blessed, but He won't force His blessings on you? He lets you choose! When you believe in His love for you and when you receive His promises and do the things He tells you -- you are choosing His blessings. He wants others to see His blessing in your life. He wants you to be blessed so that you can bless others. You are a kid of the King! Kings' kids are different from those in the world, aren't they? They are very blessed and they are expected to live a life that fits being a King's kid! Is that what you choose?

B. GOD WANTS YOU TO BE HEALTHY

1.   Exodus 15:26

God does not want us to suffer with disease. He wants us to be healthy and healed.

What did God call Himself?_____

2.   1 Peter 2:24

When Jesus died on the cross he took our sins, and by His wounds we are_____

3.   Proverbs 4:20-22

What are we supposed to pay close attention to?_____

How are we to listen?_____

If we let God's Word penetrate deep into our hearts, what will it bring to us?

_____

4.   Proverbs 12:18

Your words can bring healing to you or to others.

What kind of words don't bring healing?_____

What do the words of the wise bring?_____

5.   Proverbs 15:4

What kind of words bring life and health?_____

Can you think of an example of this kind of words?_____

What kind of words wouldn't be gentle?_____

6.   Proverbs 16:24

What type of words bring health to the body and sweetness to your soul – (your mind and emotions)?

_____

7.   Proverbs 18:21

The words of your tongue can bring_____ or_____

C.   GOD WANTS YOU TO HAVE A WEALTHY, ENJOYABLE LIFE

1.   Deuteronomy 8:18

Who gives the power to become rich?_____

What are we to remember?_____

2.   Philippians 4:19

What will God supply?_____

3.   Malachi 3:10

What does God want us to give to Him?_____

What will God do for us?_____

4.   Luke 6:38

What are we to do?_____

What will happen if we become giving people?_____

What type of things can we give to people? _____

Have you thought of giving compliments, smiles, friendly notes, any of your toys, candy or other things that are valuable to you? Did you know that lots of kids are selfish? They are thinking, "me" and "mine". They are not thinking about sharing! But, if you will learn to share the things you have with others and be a generous giver when you are a kid, the Lord will bless your life. He will be sure you have more than enough stuff!

5.   Proverbs 11:25

Who prospers?_____

6.   2 Corinthians 9:6-8

We can give a little or we can give a lot! God compares our giving to a farmer planting seeds. If a farmer plants a few corn seeds, how big will his corn crop be? If a farmer plants a lot of corn seeds, how big will his corn harvest be?

When we give, what should our attitude be?_____

Should we feel pressured to give?_____

What does God love?_____

D.   THE SECRET TO LIVING LIFE TO THE MAX

Deuteronomy 29:9

Remember these two words: Listen & Obey!

If we will listen to God and His Word and then obey the things He tells us, we will live an abundant life to the max! Remember you have to choose!

You will prosper in everything you do, if you will do what?_____

E.   JUST DO IT – TAKE ACTION

Now it's time to just do it! Let's take action on what we have studied. I want you to take a few moments to think about your relationship with the Lord. Is there any area of your life in which God has asked you to do something? To not do something? For example: Has He told you to obey your parents? Has He told you to forgive others? Has He told you to love people? Has He told you to honor your teacher? Has He told you to quit saying certain bad words? Has He told you to be generous toward others? Has He asked you to give something to someone else to bless them? Has He asked you to apologize? In your conscience, is there any area of your life that God wants you to correct because right now that area is not pleasing to the Lord?

Are you willing to obey the Lord in these areas? Are you ready to choose life? God wants you to live the life He blesses and it begins with you making good choices.

MY PERSONAL WALK WITH GOD
Pages You Can Personalize!

<u>All Things Are Possible, So Here's What I'd Do...</u>

If I had a million dollars...I would buy...

If I could fly...I would fly to....

If I could be anything when I grow up...here's what I would be...

If I could help anyone...here's who I would help...

If I could have my dreams come true...here's what I dream...

CHAPTER 11
Being A Winner
"How to be an Overcomer"

Ever felt like a major geek? Ever been mad at yourself? Have you ever felt defeated? Did you ever feel like a failure in school? Have you felt ugly? Have you felt lonely? Did you ever do something totally embarrassing? Have you ever felt sad or mad toward your friends? Ever felt like you were not included in the group? Felt rejected? Like a loser? We all face hard times. Facing hard times is a normal part of life, but God wants us as Christians to know how to trust God so that we get up, shake ourselves off and follow the Lord as He leads us to victory. As we walk through life, there will sometimes be roadblocks. Sometimes we will face challenges or difficulties that the Lord wants to help us win. These roadblocks and challenges sometimes come because we made a dumb choice, sometimes the devil tries to put difficulties in our path, and sometimes just because we live in the world we will face trouble. The good news is that no matter what you face, with God's help He can show you how to win. Jesus has made a way for us to have the victory in every area of our lives. Sometimes we will have to be patient and fight the fight of faith while God is leading us to victory, but in the end you will win because God has made you a winner!

Have you ever played tennis, video games, snowboarding, skiing, skateboarding or some other type of individual sport? Before the game, did you begin to picture the game and your strategy and how you were going to be the winner? Have you pictured yourself hitting perfect tennis shots in a really hard tennis game? Have you pictured yourself snowboarding or skiing down a hill and carving every giant, Olympic-sized mogul just perfectly? Have you imagined yourself doing skateboarding tricks at the X Games and landing every one just perfect? In order to win, you have to begin to see yourself as a winner. We are going to face pressures, opponents and Olympic-sized problems, but God wants us to imagine ourselves winning through every difficulty.

A.   GOD SEES US AS WINNERS

How does God see us as winners? We need to see ourselves that way God sees us!

1.   Romans 8:31, 37

Who is always for us, on our side?_____

If God is for us, who can be against us?_____

2.   1 Corinthians 15:57

Who do we give thanks to?_____

What does He always give us?_____

We have victory through who?_____

3.   2 Corinthians 2:14

Who do we give thanks to?_____

How often do we triumph or have the victory?_____

4.   1 John 5:4-5

Are you a child of God?_____

What will God always give you?_____

Who wins the battle?_____

5.   Psalm 34:19

Who faces troubles?_____

What does the Lord do for us?_____

6.   Philippians 4:13

How many things can I do through Christ?_____

What does God give me?_____

Don't try to do things in your own strength. You can't give yourself the victory – only God can do that as you trust Him. Always remember that God is on your side - you have

Jesus giving you victory and the Holy Spirit who helps you in all you do. You are on a winning team and God calls you a winner! God's team always wins!

B. THE WINNING TEAM

The Bible tells us that there are two kingdoms, or we could say two teams: the kingdom of light, or God's kingdom, and the kingdom of darkness, or Satan's kingdom. These two kingdoms, or teams are against each other. Jesus died on a cross so that all of us who were in Satan's kingdom of darkness could be switched to God's team - the kingdom of light. Jesus went to the cross so we could be drafted and picked up to be on God's team!

1.   Colossians 1:13

What "team" did God rescue us from?_____

What "team" has God brought us into?_____

2.   John 10:10

Jesus told us what His purpose is. What does Jesus want to bring you?_____

Satan's goal is different. What three things does Satan do?

_____   _____   _____

C. WE HAVE GOD'S POWER

God sees us as winners in Christ. God has placed us on His winning team. He wants us to act like winners and He wants us to stop our enemy from having any influence in our lives. Satan wanted to be God. He lost! The devil wants to be god in different areas of our lives, and it's our job to kick him out! We need to ignore the devil's suggestions and tell him that we are going to obey God! Let's look at the power God has given to us in Jesus.

1.   Satan Does Not Want Us To Know About Our Power

    a.   1 Peter 5:8,9

        What does the devil want to do?_____

        What are we supposed to do?_____

    b.   2 Corinthians 2:11

        God does not want Satan to outsmart us.

        What are we to be familiar with?_____

        If you want to know what the devil's evil schemes are, you can look up these verses. We can see what type of tricks the devil is up to when we read these verses. John 8:44, John 10:10, Revelation 12:10, 1 Peter 5:8, 2 Corinthians 11:14, Acts 10:38, Mark 4:15, Luke 22:31

2.   Jesus Wants Us To Know About Our Power

    a.   Luke 10:19

        What did Jesus give us?_____

        Whose power is greater – Jesus' power or the devil's power?_____

        What can hurt me?_____

    b.   1 John 4:4

        Who is in us?_____

        Who is greater?_____

        Remember you have God living inside of you! You and God are a majority! You are never alone, but the Almighty God lives inside of you and He is greater than any enemy you'll ever face!

c.   Revelation 17:14

Who is Lord of lords?_____

Who is King of kings?_____

Who wins?_____

What does God say about us - His chosen ones?_____

Jesus is the King and we are the kings. Jesus is the Lord and we are the lords. Jesus defeats the devil! He gives us His victory. Jesus gave us weapons to use to enforce Satan's defeat. Let's see what weapons God has given us.

D.   GOD HAS GIVEN US WEAPONS

1.   Hebrews 4:12 – God's Word Is A Weapon

What kind of weapon is God's word compared to?_____

When we know, believe and quote God's Word, it's just like sticking a dagger into the devil. He hates God's Word and it's one of our strong weapons!

2.   Luke 10:17, Philippians 2:9,10 – Jesus' Name Is A Weapon

Who has to bow down when we use Jesus' Name?_____

Every name has to bow down to Jesus' Name. The devil and his demons are paralyzed when we use Jesus' Name.

3.   Philippians 4:8 – Using Our Mind To Think About God's Word Is A Weapon

What are we to make our minds think about?_____

It is really important for us to be very careful about what we think. If we have a bad or evil thought, we immediately need to replace that thought with a thought from God. If we think of the things the devil wants us to think about – like scary things, evil things, bad things, fearful things, disobedient things, curse words, harmful things, illegal things, stealing, killing, and naughty things - our minds will be filled with fear and confusion. These kinds of thoughts can even give us bad dreams. If we think of the things God wants us to think about – like loving people, being nice, being generous, obeying our parents, being respectful to our teachers and adults, happy things, fun things, pure things – our minds will be filled with peace and joy. These kinds of thoughts give us a happy life!

 WHAT TO DO WITH YOUR THOUGHTS: What do you do if you have a bad thought? You replace it! Here's an example. What if I tell you to think about a pink elephant. What are you now thinking of? A pink elephant, right? What if I told you to stop thinking about the pink elephant, could you? It would be hard to just stop thinking of the pink elephant. Instead of trying to stop thinking of a thought, you need to replace the thought with something else. So, what if I said to replace your thought of the pink elephant with a thought of a red dog. Now what are you thinking about? You are thinking about a red dog, right? By replacing our bad thoughts with good thoughts from God's Word, we can control our thoughts to be in line with God's desire. This is a great weapon to use when the devil tries to give you his thoughts – just replace the devil's thoughts with God's thoughts!

E. JUST DO IT – TAKE ACTION

Now it's time to just do it! Let's take action on what we have studied. God has made you winner! He has put you on His winning team! God has given you power and weapons so that you can always win! Thank God for Jesus, His shed blood on the cross, the Word of God and the Name of Jesus! Be sure to focus your thoughts on God's Word, and you will live the life of victory on God's winning team no matter how hard your opponent fights against you – you are a winner!

MY PERSONAL WALK WITH GOD
Pages You Can Personalize!

Who Are Your Favorite Winners? Do you know?

Who's your favorite preacher?

Do you have a favorite Bible character? Who and why?

If you were a missionary, what country would you want to live in?

What is your favorite sport?

Who is your favorite hockey, baseball, football or basketball team?

Who was the quarterback of the winning team in the Super Bowl?

Who is the best golfer?

Who is the top tennis player for women and men?

Do you know the name of a NASCAR driver?

What sports have you played?

If you were a professional athlete,
what sport would you play and which team would you like to play with?

CHAPTER 12
Serving God
"How To Be Used By God"

God has a job for you to do! Did you know that? He has a special plan for you. He knows you better than anyone and He wants the very best for your life. It's important to know the path God wants you to follow so that you can walk right into His best plan for you. You can't get this plan from anyone else and you can't copy others; you just need to follow God from your heart. Let's look at this.

A. YOU ARE GOD'S MINISTER

Did you know that you are already a minister? Maybe you aren't called "Pastor" or "Reverend", but you are a minister for God!

1.   2 Corinthians 5:18

What task has God given you?_____

What do you think "reconciliation" means?_____

RECONCILIATION: This is a big word which means "restoration to divine favor." In modern language, we would say, since Jesus died on the cross to pay for our sins, God wants people to know that He is not mad at them and He wants to be friends with them.

God has a job for you to do! Let's look at some of the jobs God asks His children to do.

2.   1 Corinthians 12:28

Did you know God has placed us in His family right where He wants us? In verse 28, He describes some of the jobs God wants different people to do. Do you see the list? Besides "healing", what other ministry starts with an "H"?

"those who can _____ others."

The first job you get to do for God is to simply help others! It's called the ministry of helps! Look at the people in your family, your friends, schoolmates and the people at church and see if there are ways you can help others. This is your first ministry – helping others!

3.   Matthew 20:26-28

If you want to be great in God's kingdom and if you want to be a leader, what must you do?

_____

Even Jesus didn't come to be served, but to do what?_____

How could you serve your family and friends better?_____

4.   Mathew 7:12

How should you treat others?_____

5.   John 6:5-13

Let's look at a young boy that God used as His minister. This boy gave Jesus what he had and Jesus performed a miracle!

What did the little boy give?

Five barley _____   Two small _____

In verse 10, how many men were present and fed?_____

Before Jesus passed out the food, what did He do?_____

How many baskets were filled after everyone ate?_____

B.   YOU ARE GOD'S MESSENGER

1.   Mark 16:15

       What did Jesus tell us to do?_____

2.   Matthew 5:14-16

       What did Jesus call you?_____

       What are we supposed to do with our light?_____

       When we do good deeds, our light is shining and people see our Heavenly Father
       in our lives!

       Can you think of a good deed that you've done recently?_____

3.   Matthew 4:19

       Who does Jesus want you to follow?_____

       What will Jesus make you to become?_____

LUKE'S STORY: *Did you know that even as a kid, you can share Jesus with your friends? One day, when my son Luke was in third grade he told me that he shared Jesus with a boy on the playground during recess. He asked his friend is he knew Jesus and if he wanted to go to heaven. His friend said he didn't know Jesus. Luke explained a little about Jesus and going to heaven and he asked his friend if he would like to invite Jesus into his life and his friend said "yes"! Luke prayed with his friend right there on the playground and he received Jesus into his heart. God can use kids to share the good news of Jesus!*

ERIC & LUKE'S STORY: *One year we had a special outreach Easter Service at our church. We wanted to invite our friends and neighbors to attend, so Eric and Luke got on their bicycles and delivered invitations to our neighbors. It was a simple way to help spread the good news of Jesus! Have you thought of inviting your friends and neighbors to your church?*

C. GOD HAS A GOOD PLAN FOR YOUR LIFE

1. Jeremiah 29:11

   What kind of plan does God have for your life?_____

2. Ephesians 2:10

   What does God call you?_____

   What has God planned for us to do?_____

3. 1 Peter 4:10

   What has God given to you?_____

   If we discover these gifts and use them, what can flow through us?_____

   As you grow up, you will begin to notice certain talents and gifts that God has given you. Are you a good speaker or actor who loves to talk in front of people? Are you gifted to draw or write or create things? Maybe you are gifted in sports or in building things. Maybe you are an organizer or a real people friendly type person. Each person has special gifts and talents from God. We are all unique and special, and once we understand our gifts and talents, we will be able to use them to serve God in a special way.

D. JUST DO IT - TAKE ACTION

Now it's time to just do it! Let's take action on what we have studied. It's time to pray and think about serving God by helping someone in your life!

Let's think, if you were going to do something nice and helpful for one person, so that they could know God's love, which person would you pick?

_____

What nice thing do you want to do for this person?_____

When will you do it?_____

MY PERSONAL WALK WITH GOD
Pages You Can Personalize!

These Are My Family, Friends & Neighbors...
I Am Going To Pray For Them And
Look For A Way To Share Jesus With Them

Name:_____

Name:_____

Name:_____

Name:_____

Name:_____

Name:_____

These Are Missionaries I Want To Pray For:

Name:_____

Name:_____

Name:_____

Name:_____

CONGRATULATIONS!

You did it! You've completed "Getting A Grip On The Basics For Kids"!

Now, you have the rest of your life to get to know your Heavenly Father, Jesus your Lord and the Holy Spirit your Helper even better! We pray for God's very best in your life as you follow Him!

ABOUT THE AUTHOR

Beth Jones has been helping people 'get the basics' of God's Word for over thirty years. She is the author of over twenty books, including the popular Getting A Grip On The Basics Bible study series being used by thousands of churches in America and abroad. She hosts The Basics With Beth TV program aired around the world and she and her husband Jeff founded and serve as the senior pastors of Valley Family Church in Kalamazoo, Michigan.

For more resources from Beth or to contact her ministry, just go to:
thebasicswithbeth.com